C O U N T

COUNTRY STYLE

Villa • *Maison* • *Casa* • *Cottage*

ELIZABETH HILLIARD

PHOTOGRAPHS BY JOHN MILLER

PAVILION

Originally published in Great Britain as
Cottage (1994), *Maison* (1994),
Villa (1995) and *Casa* (1995) by
Pavilion Books Limited
London House, Great Eastern Wharf
Parkgate Road, London SW11 4NQ

This edition published in 1998 by
Pavilion Books Limited

Copyright Elizabeth Hilliard 1994, 1995
Photographs copyright John Miller 1994, 1995

The moral right of the author has been asserted

Designed by Write Image Limited

A CIP catalogue record for this book is available from the
British Library

ISBN 1 86205 179 8

Printed and bound in Singapore by Imago

2 4 6 8 10 9 7 5 3 1

This book may be ordered by post direct from the publisher. Please
contact the Marketing Department. But try your bookshop first.

CONTENTS

A typical Tuscan jar with handles is a useful container for cooking implements. The flat 'spoon' with wooden prongs is used for stirring strands of pasta to loosen them in boiling water.

VILLA
Italian Country Style

ITALIAN COUNTRY STYLE IS A DELICIOUS MIXTURE OF TRADITIONS. DIFFERENCES IN cultural heritage and climate have given every region of this seductively beautiful country an identity and vernacular style of its own.

Just as building materials vary from one place to another, so methods of construction are adapted to suit the very different needs of local people. While a cedar-wood chalet in the Dolomites, for example, is built to keep out the snow, a white-painted stone *trullo* in Puglia – seven hundred miles south – is built to reflect the glare of the sun. The chalet undoubtedly has more in common with others across the border in Austria, the *trullo* with buildings in Greece, than either of them shares with houses the length of the peninsula in between. These contrasts mean not only that Italian country style is rich in local influences but also that it can be defined in a number of ways.

The vast majority of visitors to the Italian countryside flock to the central regions – Tuscany, principally, with an overflow into Umbria, the Marche and Lazio – and the domestic style most readily associated with Italy in the minds of foreigners is that of the stone-built central Italian villa or farmhouse. *Italian Country Style* reflects this tendency, devoting most of its pages to these regions, whose landscape, climate and way of life have produced, with minor variations, a distinct, and homogeneous style.

As a counterbalance, and as a demonstration of Italy's spectacular contrasts, a house in the far north of the country, at Cortina d'Ampezzo, is also included. Famous as a ski resort, Cortina, in Trentino-Alto Adige, is the capital of the Dolomites, often said to be the most beautiful mountains in the world. Here the climate is a more powerful influence than any other on the building style of the region. Typically, the older houses are constructed of a combination of wood and local stone, sometimes with superb lattice-work decoration on their upper storeys. Roofs are steeply pitched and overhang the walls by several feet to shed melting snow well away from the house. External wooden balconies running the length of south-facing walls make it possible, even in winter, to take a little exercise and enjoy the sun. In summer the carved balustrades of these balconies are festooned with baskets of flowers.

Internally, too, the walls, floors and ceilings of houses are constructed of wood to provide insulation. Antique furniture tends to be ornate compared with that of many other country districts, showing off the skill of local carpenters. As in any northern region, keeping warm in winter is a preoccupation; here the problem is often solved by a wood-burning stove. Some are magnificent – huge and highly decorative. Since they serve to heat the entire house, they are usually centrally sited in the kitchen.

One vital element that is common to country houses throughout Italy is the importance of the kitchen. For the *contadini*, or tenant farmers, of the past, the main event of the day, when all the family gathered together, was *pranzo*, or lunch. In the farmhouses of the central regions this was often eaten in a vast kitchen in which the only source of comfort was a wood fire burning on an enormous hearth. This leads to a central point about Italian country style: the family is the focus of everything. Italian households rich and poor revolve around the family; the arrangement and size of rooms, as well as their decoration, are geared to the family's essential social activities.

A detail of the fireplace illustrated on page 59, showing the putto's *head and wings.*

Outside walls in the lanes of towns and villages around Florence are often finished with decorative graffiti incised into the rough plaster. Made with a tool formed from nails hammered into a stick of wood, the patterns are wonderfully fresh because the artisan had only about twenty minutes before each panel of new plaster became too dry to work. This graffiti is unusual because it is indoors.

———————————

In the past, three or four generations lived together under one roof, and, though this is nowadays a rarity, far fewer Italians than Anglo-Saxons live alone. Even newly married couples often live with one or other set of parents for reasons of economy and convenience. The idea of privacy has until recently had little significance; even the word, *la privacy*, is new and imported.

If the family is the focus of life, the hearth is the symbol of family unity. In almost every traditional farmhouse, or *casa colonica*, the kitchen is dominated by a massive fireplace, watched over by the *nonna*, or grandmother, to ensure that the precious wood doesn't burn up too fast. In the past, heavy, blackened cauldrons, in which water was boiled and pasta was cooked for the midday meal, would have been suspended over the flames. Pasta is still made at home by many Italians, if only on special occasions, and every traditional kitchen has its pasta board and array of pasta-making utensils. A link with kitchens across the western world is provided by the familiar two-tier Moka coffee maker, which went into mass production after the Second World War. The Art Deco faceting on this delectable gadget makes it look like something between a Cubist's reinterpretation of the kettle and a lunar module. It is a design classic whose fresh, modern look belies its age. Without it no Italian kitchen would be complete.

Pre-war rural customs, especially where cookery is concerned, continue almost unchanged in many parts of Italy today. They are kept alive not just by *contadini* but also by middle-class country-house owning Italians who relish the chance to enjoy genuine, unpretentious country food.

The early decades of the twentieth century saw a considerable movement of Italians to North and South America, among other places, in search of work. Even today there are towns in such alien environments as the north of England where a restaurant or *trattoria* is almost entirely staffed by young men from the particular village in Italy whence the proprietor hails. In the 1950s and 1960s another exodus occurred as young people began to reject the hard work of life on the land in favour of more lucrative jobs in the cities. The farmhouses their families had inhabited for generations were gradually abandoned and fell into disrepair. As the market for such houses developed, so they began to come on the market, and in recent years Belgians, Germans, Dutch and umpteen others have joined the British in the rush for a rural idyll, with the result that every dilapidated tower and rustic haybarn from Liguria to Lazio is now being snapped up and converted.

The idea of doing up a place in the country is relatively new to the Italian professional classes. But Rome, Milan and other centres have become so chaotic in the past ten years that many people are now finding life intolerable without a bolt hole in the country to which they can retreat. Ilaria Miani is an example of an Italian who has caught the renovation bug. She and her family escape from Rome, where she has a business making reproduction antique furniture, to a farmhouse with stunning views over the Val d'Orcia, west of Montepulciano, the fourth house they have restored. 'The British, amongst other foreigners, really saw the potential in Tuscany and restored villas and farmhouses here', says Signora Miani. 'We owe them a great debt, though few Italians would like to admit it!'

Except in the most fashionable parts of Tuscany and Umbria, there is no shortage of desirable relics in agricultural areas. This is especially true of the south of Italy, or *Mezzogiorno*. But the trend is showing signs of slowing if not reversing as farming becomes more mechanized and modern housing more readily available. This new tendency does not, however, threaten the choice offered to someone looking for an old farmhouse, olive mill or granary to do up, as the type of home in demand from the local population is usually as new on the outside as it is easy-care on the inside.

Two magnificent pottery jugs of peasant design with wonderful depth and variation of colour in their glazes stand on a mid-nineteenth-century chest of drawers from the Veneto region of Italy.

Surrounded by a cluster of ancient outbuildings, the archetypal Italian farmhouse of everyone's dreams stands four-square on a Tuscan hilltop with a view over its own olive groves and vineyards that have scarcely changed since the fourteenth century. No wonder the idea of owning such a place has an irresistible appeal. The reality is that a country house or cow byre ripe for conversion will very likely have no mains water, road or sanitation. A building of any age and substance will, however, share some of the features common to the most beautiful examples of central Italian country style. It will be built of mellow local stone and roofed with lichen-covered *coppi* (the curved earthenware roof tiles to be found throughout the Mediterranean); its win-

A ceiling formed from pianelle, *thin bricks used for roofing (as here) or as a base for an upstairs floor, in which case terracotta tiles are placed on the bricks.*

dows and doors, in the better buildings at least, will be framed in *travertine* or *pietra serena* (two types of dressed local stone), perhaps with faded shutters still intact; and it will form an integral part of the landscape to which it belongs.

Construction work is frequently overseen by a *geometra*, a man (almost invariably) who acts as site manager for an architect, combining some of the skills and knowledge of an architect and a surveyor with an invaluable understanding of the rules and regulations governing the restoration of old buildings. 'The rules seem to change every time we come out!' says one British owner of a renovated Tuscan farmhouse. 'The Italian authorities have woken up to conservation and are strict about your not altering the outside of old houses and even, sometimes, the inside. But we didn't find them officious or aggressive.'

The typical *casa colonica* is muscular, classically proportioned and uncompromising. Cosy it is not. Designed for coolness in the long, hot summers, its stone walls are

often two feet (60cm) thick. The rooms are vast and unadorned, often the only orna-
ment being a plastercast of the Madonna high on a wall. Since the *contadini* rarely owned
the buildings in which they lived, had very little money and spent most of the hours of
daylight out of doors, there was little incentive to embellish them. Furniture was mini-
mal and often home made. When it broke it was either repaired with whatever came
to hand or thrown away. As a result there is relatively little good antique country furniture in Italy compared with Britain, for example, where tenant farmers gained their
independence much earlier, and, with it, a pride in home ownership. What there is is
expensive. However, a good traditional piece, such as a panelled *cassapanca* (large chest)
or *armadio* (wardrobe), originally the property of a country landowner, has the sort of
integrity and simplicity that epitomize Italian country house style.

The most highly prized item of furniture in any Tuscan or Umbrian farmer's house
was the matrimonial bed. This was an elaborate affair, traditionally made of wrought
iron, the head decorated with curvilinear shapes framing a large, painted oval medal-
lion depicting the Madonna or a local saint in a wreath of flowers. Today such beds
are more likely to be found in the country homes of foreigners or city escapees, eager
to adopt the trappings of a vanishing rural lifestyle, than in the houses of local people,
who have long since discarded them in favour of modern mass-produced alternatives.

Another traditional piece of furniture now finding its way back to Tuscan and
Umbrian farmhouses is the *madia*, a sort of chest on legs which was used in the past as
a kneading trough for the making of bread. (Nowadays it more often serves as a drinks
cabinet or cutlery store.) Almost all old country furniture that has survived the rav-
ages of time is made of local chestnut, a weather-resistant and beautiful hardwood
that is still used for the making of doors, window frames and furniture. Most houses
would have had one or two cupboards built into the thickness of the walls of the kitchen

15

to store food and crockery, a large table, a motley collection of wooden chairs, a stool or two by the fire and a few simple chests for clothes, linen and valuables. In the way of furniture they would have had little else.

Even as a weekend or holiday retreat, most city-dwellers would regard such simplicity as spartan, and have introduced the sort of creature comforts they are used to at home: easy chairs and settees, for instance, which are almost unknown in a *contadino* house. Nonetheless, the spacious, symmetrical rooms of Italian farmhouses lend themselves to being under furnished, and the simpler the furniture the more dramatic it looks against the granular, plastered walls.

Chairs are often arranged round the edge of the room rather than grouped in the middle, lending Italian country style a slightly formal air and a sense of organization. This has allowed it to assimilate elements of the clean-cut look which has made modern Italian fashion, furniture and household goods famous the world over: stylish lamps, for example, and the wonderfully elegant coffee pots designed by Alessi. In this way, new country house owners can have the best of both worlds, enjoying the textures of an ancient building and the products of local craftsmanship without sacrificing the convenience of labour-saving gadgetry or the beauty of modern Italian design.

A thrusting, city-dwelling couple, whose urban apartment is sleek and high-tech, will arrive at their country place and relax with a sigh of relief and a glass of red wine. Their *soggiorno*, or living room, like the rest of the house, is decorated to look unpretentious but smart in an understated way. Country style is relaxing because it is not intended to impress anyone; it is primarily for one's own comfort and enjoyment.

In most old farmhouses massive, hand-sawn chestnut beams support the ceilings, with narrower beams, or correntini, laid transversely to carry the weight of the floor tiles of the upper rooms. The most usual type of flooring is terracotta tiles – rectangular or,

On a fireplace mantelshelf stand two handsome pewter jars, inscribed with the initials of the owner and the date.
These were used for transporting water or, more probably, wine on hunting trips.

less frequently, hexagonal in shape – with a scattering of rugs to soften and warm them in winter. Italy is the largest importer in the world, relative to its population, of Turkish and Persian carpets. In summer, terracotta floors are often left bare to show off the beauty of their surface, smoothed to a soft sheen by the passage of feet and

An old chest with iron straps, handles and clasp stands sturdily on weathered terracotta tiles.

undulating with age. In more modern houses and apartments, terrazzo tiling (marble chips laid in a mortar and highly polished) has largely taken over from terracotta as it is considered a great deal easier to keep clean.

Most buildings in central and southern Italy have window shutters, frequently louvred, to filter the sun, and in the traditional *casa colonica* curtains are a rarity. Many foreign owners, however, particularly those from northern Europe, find bare window frames a little stark, and plain, unbleached calico or linen curtains can enhance the comfort of a room without detracting from its simplicity. For bed coverings and upholstery the subtle, earthy tones of vegetable-dyed fabrics are the perfect complement to the faded ochres and terracotta shades of the building itself.

Some of the grander and more elegant country houses have summer and winter drawing rooms, decorated in appropriate colours, the summer room pale and airy, the winter one furnished in darker, richer colours and with a fireplace as its focus. In addition there are smaller, more intimate rooms where the family gathers and friends are received.

Dilapidated farm buildings are ideal villa fodder in the sense that you can make pretty well what you want of a wreck. A significant distinguishing characteristic of proponents of country style, however, be they Italian, British or other, is their concern for a certain degree of authenticity. Ilaria Miani's team used construction stone which had tumbled from the crumbling building and was found in the undergrowth around the house, and interior walls were repaired using lime mortar. Although such skills as high quality stone masonry and the making of lime mortar have practically died out in many areas, it is still possible to find craftsmen willing and able to practise them, especially in central Italy where traditional materials and methods are in demand by the new wave of country house owners.

The Mianis found antique tiles for the upstairs and downstairs floors, and fittings large and small, from beams to doorknobs, to replace those stolen during the quarter century that the house was empty. Rooms have been simply painted, with wide bands of flat colour along the bottoms of walls and around doors. In many as yet unconverted houses the original tempera paint – strong pinks and blues for the most part – still clings to the peeling plaster of the walls, with a band of a darker colour below; this band is known as the *battiscopa* and served to disguise the marks left by the broom hitting the wall when sweeping the floor.

Despite a general desire for authenticity, there is one way in which old farmhouses throughout the country are almost invariably radically altered in the course of conversion. The ground floor originally served as a *stalla*, or cowshed; people lived upstairs. *Stalle* are now being turned into living rooms, complete with fireplaces, and kitchens

An elaborate closet for linen in a house in Cortina d'Ampezzo. The hand-carved panelling was made in 1941 from wood from the Arolla pine, Pinus cembra, *which grows in the area, and is finished with wax polish.*

are being moved from upstairs to downstairs. In the larger farmhouses, especially in the central regions, a striking feature of the *stalle* is often the magnificent brick-ribbed arches spanning the crypt-like interior space. Once converted, the ground floor provides a dramatic open-plan living area, sometimes using the wood from the *mangiatoio*, or manger – rubbed smooth by years of wear by feeding cattle – to make beautiful shelves or benches. Staircases, which were external and usually roofed, served only to provide access to living quarters upstairs.

At the Villa Cesia, near Rome, built between the eleventh and the fifteenth centuries, and restored in the twentieth by fashion designer Laura Biagiotti, the Milanese architect-designer Piero Pinto made the exciting discovery that there had been an internal staircase in former times, though the lower part had been filled in with earth. In other houses the architect has to juggle practical necessity with aesthetic and historical considerations to create a staircase and passages where there were none before.

In summer, outdoor space close to the house is used as an extra room, linked to the living rooms by french doors or, in modern conversions, by large expanses of sliding glass. One of the greatest delights of life here, as in all Mediterranean countries, is an *al fresco* lunch with family and friends under the dappled shade of a pergola dripping with grapes or wisteria.

The appeal of Italian country style is due, in no small part, to its application of traditional skills and materials to the demands of modern living. Walk into a house in rural Italy and you will feel a sense of ease in its well-proportioned rooms, and a timelessness that emanates from its classical simplicity and its relationship to the surrounding landscape.

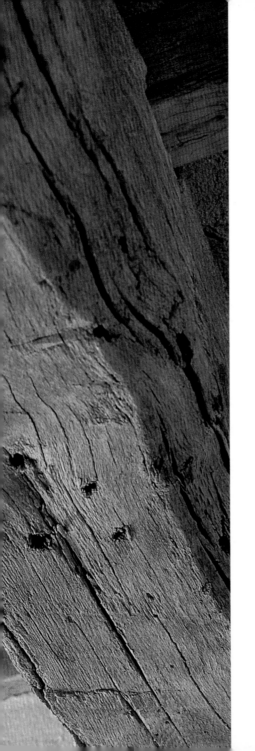

FLOORS, STAIRS & CEILINGS

THE FLOORS AND CEILINGS OF COUNTRY HOUSES IN ITALY ARE ROBUST AND UNPRETENTIOUS. A GRAND VILLA HAS TERRACOTTA TILES ON THE FLOOR, AND SO DOES A CONVERTED TUSCAN FARMHOUSE. SPLENDID WOODEN BEAMS SUPPORT CEILINGS AND ROOFS; SOLID STAIRCASES CARRY YOU FROM ONE FLOOR TO THE NEXT.

The ceiling of this downstairs room is made from large oak beams and smaller joists, on which are arranged thin bricks called pianelle. *The floor of the bedroom above is formed from terracotta tiles laid on these bricks.*

A stone staircase with painted iron balusters leads to the attics of a villa in the country near Florence, the summer home of an aristocratic family. The colour of the paint was popular at the end of the nineteenth century.

A newly formed indoor staircase in a renovated farmhouse. When the ground level of a farm building was inhabited by animals, the farmer and his family reached the upper floor by an outdoor staircase, today replaced by staircases such as this one.

The warm colour and worn appearance of these reclaimed terracotta tiles suggest centuries of use and have enduring appeal not only in the Italian countryside. The fashion for reclaimed terracotta means that such tiles are being rescued and exported for sale in countries across the world.

*This type of Italian country kitchen, with a floor of reclaimed terracotta tiles, is not only practical and beautiful,
but also inspires people all over the world to install 'farmhouse' kitchens of their own.*

Above. *A ceiling contrasting with the one on pages 22–3, here constructed from sturdy beams, joists and planks instead of* pianelle, *thin bricks.*
Right. *The entire ceiling above the Tyrolean bed is whitewashed, beams and all.*

A vault constructed from terracotta tiles over a bathroom window. This room was formerly a pigsty, when the lower floor of the building was inhabited by animals and the upper floor by the farmer and his family.

DOORS & WINDOWS

EXTERNAL DOORS ARE ROBUST, INTERNAL DOORS DELICATE AND OFTEN ELEGANT. WINDOWS ARE DESIGNED TO PROTECT THE INTERIOR FROM THE BRILLIANT SUMMER SUNLIGHT, EITHER BY USE OF SMALL OPENINGS, WOODEN INTERIOR SHUTTERS OR, INTRIGUINGLY, BY CLEVER USE OF A PATTERN OF TERRACOTTA TILES SET ON THEIR ENDS AT ANGLES.

A heavy old door connecting one part of the terrace with another, in a wall roughly built of brick and stone. Originally painted a traditional strong green, it has faded in the sun to this shade of salvia, *or sage green.*

A magnificent, heavy wooden front door with iron bolts and hinges which would have been made by the local blacksmith. This example was found in a builders' yard, reclaimed and installed in a house which is part thirteenth century, part eighteenth century.

A bedroom door, again a simple affair made from planks painted with limewash and furnished with typically Tuscan ironmongery.

In 1929 this villa was redecorated and the door painted with pastoral scenes and an urn above. The artist was local and the decorations, which were standard in grand houses, were in a style popular from the end of the eighteenth century until well into the twentieth.

Terracotta tiles up-ended in a geometric pattern fill the outside of the kitchen window embrasure. Inside it is glazed, with the tiles creating shade from the sun without obscuring the view from the kitchen sink.

The restorers of this farmhouse have taken trouble to ensure that new windows are small, in keeping with the building's history. Peasant farmers did not want large window openings, making the house cold in winter and hot in summer. This casement opens inwards, and has glass in the panes and an interior shutter attached to the frame.

PAINT

PAINTED COLOUR IS USED IN MANY
FLAMBOYANT WAYS IN ITALIAN COUNTRY
HOUSES. IT PROVIDES ACCENTS ON WALLS
AND AROUND DOORS AND WINDOWS;
PAINTED DECORATION ENLIVENS THE
FORMS OF ANTIQUE FURNITURE; AND THE
LAYERS ARE SCRUBBED AWAY ON SIMPLE
PEASANT FURNITURE TO REVEAL DECADES
OF DIFFERENT COLOURS.

*Appealingly distressed paintwork on an old cupboard
reveals the many colours of paint applied over
decades of use.*

A shelf, formed from a niche in a wall, stores and displays wall paint used to decorate around doors, windows and this niche itself. The paints are traditional limewashes tinted with pigment. They have separated over time but the components mix again quickly if stirred, and these samples are kept for retouching and repairing worn areas.

Simple painted plank doors in the hall of a converted farmhouse. The hat hooks are typically Tuscan and would have been made by the village blacksmith. This interior is entirely decorated with limewash paint. White walls are enlivened by a variation on the traditional battiscopa, *a wide strip of colour along the base of the wall, intended to disguise marks made by the broom.*

Looking from one room to another, it is here possible to see at one glance several of the colours used to decorate this Tuscan farmhouse.

A piece of Indian fabric acts as a colourful tablecloth on a painted bedroom table. The floor is laid with terracotta tiles and covered with rugs, and the simple rustic chair is also painted in a contrasting red.

Like the kitchen cupboard on pages 36–7, this wardrobe has had the paint of decades scrubbed from it in such a way that the resulting effect is soft and mellow.

Above. *This marriage chest of 1873, painted with the date of the event, would have held sheets and other linen which the bride brought to her new home as part of her dowry.*

Left. *A handsome beam painted with the traditional lime-based paint which gradually flakes and peels as it ages.*

A painted wooden clock in a house in Cortina d'Ampezzo. The faux marble, flower-picture panels, decorative borders and a cut-out patterned base are typical of the Tyrol region of the Italian Alps, formerly part of Austria.

A magnificent example of a marriage wardrobe with the date of the wedding, 1830, painted on it. The delightful portraits on either side were found in a shop in Rome and show traditional Lombardy costumes of the later nineteenth century.

LIVING
SPACES

INDOORS AND OUT, LIVING SPACES IN
ITALIAN COUNTRY HOUSES ARE WELL-
ORGANIZED IN A SIMPLE, RESTRAINED
WAY WHICH BRINGS TOGETHER OLD AND
NEW POSSESSIONS. A ROOM RARELY FEELS
CROWDED WITH FURNITURE AND OBJECTS
AND USUALLY HAS LITTLE OR NO CLUTTER.
ELEGANCE AND COMFORT ARE ACHIEVED
WITH APPARENT EFFORTLESSNESS.

A bench in the hall of the house in Tuscany.
The English cotton fabric, from Designers Guild, is
used one way on the seat cushion and back-to-front
on the bolster.

An A-shaped wooden chest of drawers, typical of the Tyrolean furniture found in the Italian Alps.

*Sets of chamois horns, hunters' trophies of the early nineteenth century, hang in a
traditional geometric pattern in a house in Cortina d'Ampezzo in the Dolomite mountains
in northern Italy.*

A larger section of the fresh and bold geometric pattern incised into rough plaster (see also page 10). This pattern is unusual in that it appears in a dining room whereas such graffiti was usually seen on external walls in the lanes of towns and villages around Florence.

*A painted shutter at a window overlooking the drive of a villa in Tuscany. The
shutters are eighteenth century and the tempera (egg based) paint is original.
Decoration in this style was used all over the house and is common in other grand
villas in the area.*

Spring water gushes from the tap of a travertine marble sink on the terrace of a Tuscan farmhouse. Similar outdoor sinks were used by peasant farmers for drawing water, washing, and watering their livestock.

The terrace of a Tuscan farmhouse with the table set for a meal. This terrace has been newly created by the restorers of this farm building to provide a shady outdoor room, complete with vine-covered pergola. West-facing, it has breathtaking views over the Val d'Orcia.

FIREPLACES

———

THE FIREPLACE OR STOVE IS USUALLY
THE ONLY FORM OF HEATING IN AN
ITALIAN COUNTRY HOUSE AND IS OF VITAL
IMPORTANCE. IN WINTER SUCH HOUSES
ARE USUALLY TOO COLD FOR COMFORT
AND THE INHABITANTS DECAMP TO THE
CITY UNTIL SPRING. HOUSES IN THE
MOUNTAINS, HOWEVER, ARE BUILT TO BE
WARM IN WINTER.

*A detail of the carved wooden fireplace on page 58, its
pattern traditional and dateless.*

*A multi-tier wood-burning stove of the type which was once used for heating rooms
in superior farmhouses in the Tuscan countryside. An elaborate example in a grand
villa might have six tiers, be highly ornate and might even be glazed. The fire irons
are for* bellezza; *in fact all you need to operate the stove is a shovel.*

One of the magnificent stone buttresses supporting the stone mantel shelf over the fireplace left.

A wide open downhearth in the sitting room of a Tuscan house gives ample heat on cool days and evenings.

A warming scene in winter. The fire surround was hand carved in 1941, when this house in Cortina d'Ampezzo was fitted out, but the design is traditional to this area and is dateless. The gilded clock is early nineteenth century and was brought from Turin.

The head and wings of a putto *or cherub which looks out from a seventeenth-century limestone and marble fireplace, bought and installed in 1929. The fire is never lit in winter because the house is so cold that the family abandons it and moves to Florence.*

KITCHENS

ITALIAN FAMILY LIFE REVOLVES AROUND
MEALTIMES AND THE KITCHEN, WHICH
IS USUALLY A WELCOMING ROOM WITH A
LARGE TABLE. POTS AND PANS ARE ON
DISPLAY ON WALLS OR HANGING FROM
CEILINGS; FAMILIAR OLD FURNITURE
ADDS TO THE FRIENDLINESS OF THE
ROOM, AND FRESH VEGETABLES WAITING
FOR PREPARATION LEND SPASHES OF
BRIGHT COLOUR.

*A kitchen work surface formed from the ubiquitous
terracotta tiles, with luscious vegetables and herbs
waiting to be prepared for cooking.*

Before this farmhouse was renovated the family kitchen was a stable. Animals lived on the ground floor of such buildings and the farmer and his wife above. Traditional baskets and pans hang from the ceiling.

The owner of this kitchen found the hand-hewn stone sink in the grounds when restoring her house near Florence. The kitchen, which is predictably used for eating as well as preparing and cooking food, is decorated with hand-made tiles and plates from Amalfi, south of Naples, famous for its pottery.

A massive pine laundry cupboard in a guardaroba, *an ante room to the kitchen, in a large villa in Tuscany.*

Ripe watermelon and apples, bought in the local market, rest in nineteenth-century wooden peasant-made bowls on top of a pine kitchen cupboard.

Una madia, *literally a bread bin, but actually more of a cupboard. The front and top fold back, to provide access to the space for storing flour as well as bread.*

A traditional ham stand hanging from a beam in the kitchen. When you lay it on the counter, the feet stick up and hold the prosciutto firm for carving. This stand is modern but the same design has been in use for centuries in Italian kitchens.

Built into the walls of an eighteenth-century Tuscan house, this bread oven was operated by building a fire and pushing it to one side once it had burnt down and heated the interior. Loaves were then inserted and later removed when cooked with the flat iron shovel.

A sink made of pietra serena *in the pantry, in the late eighteenth-century part of a villa. The tiles are something of a joke in the aristocratic family whose summer home this is, because they show their coat of arms (given in 1701) back to front.*

BEDROOMS
&
BATHROOMS

In an Italian country house where the beamed bedroom ceiling is painted with traditional whitewash, you are grateful for a bed which gives you a roof over your head to protect you from falling flakes of paint. Bathrooms in converted farmhouses are always modern.

A bathroom floor covered in the early years of the twentieth century with tiles decorated in a style popular from the end of the previous century. The tiles were probably made at Impruneta, near Florence, where ceramics are still made today.

A modern interpretation of a traditional Tyrolean bed, in a house in central Italy. The height of the mattress means you can see out of the window when lying on the bed, and there is room underneath for storing things. The top of the bed protects you from flakes of paint falling from the whitewashed ceiling.

A pair of beds from Laboratorio Ilaria Miani in the Mianis' Tuscan home. Inspired by the dignified simplicity of Shaker furniture, the beds are painted and draped with Indian muslin, again to protect the sleeper from falling fragments of limewash.

A fresh and uncluttered bedroom furnished with painted pieces such as the wardrobe, and folding furniture like the butler's tray, a modern reinterpretation of a classic piece of furniture.

This magnificent polished, carved and gilded bedhead was made near Florence for Senator Ferrante Capponi, a Florentine nobleman who died in 1689. It is still in the Capponi family villa.

Alongside this closet is a small painting of a detail of northern European costume, the back of a woman's head showing her elaborate lace or crocheted cap.

A painted marriage wardrobe, brought by the bride as part of her dowry, in a bedroom in northern Italy.

Bathrooms in converted farm buildings are always, inevitably, modern. Here the bath has been surrounded with old terracotta tiles. The photograph frame is modern, based on gilded flower designs found on antique Japanese kimono boxes.

The owner of this Tuscan house has a taste for round basins. These are set into polished peperino, below mirrors with frames made at the Laboratorio Ilaria Miani in Rome. The plumbing beneath is disguised with simple painted paling.

A charming Christmas wreath of dried grasses, hung on the door of a house in the Camargue to signify joyful seasonal greetings. It is suspended by a sash of traditional Provençal fabric from Souleiado.

MAISON
French Country Style

WHEN ONE THINKS OF FRENCH COUNTRY STYLE, AN IMAGE IMMEDIATELY SPRINGS TO mind. The scene is set in the dappled shade of a plane tree near the windows of a low stone house, shutters closed against the baking heat. Brilliant, hot sunshine has already begun to bleach last year's fresh coats of rich pink paint on the outside walls and the blue of the plank shutters. A wooden table is covered with a brightly patterned cloth and has been laid for a meal, with plain white china, thick glass tumblers, simple stainless steel cutlery, and a thick, pressed linen napkin beside each place. Sounds of laughter and food preparation waft out from a door in the building beyond. You enter and find yourself in a cavernous kitchen.

The large, French country kitchen is as much a place to meet and gossip as to cook and eat – providing the chat does not distract from the serious business of cooking. The sound of corks popping from bottles of rosé and the mouthwatering scents of cooking garlic, rosemary and the classic Provençal ratatouille accompany you as you make your way around the room. You notice the row of copper pans hanging on the wall – gleaming russet-gold vessels in a dozen sizes, each with its own special purpose.

You move on to admire shelves weighed down with local faience and marbled pottery, the magnificent wide cooker, beneath the canopy of the kitchen's vast fireplace,

The collection of eggy objects on these kitchen shelves was inspired by the fine metal wirework of the baskets on the top shelf, which date from around 1900.

bearing bubbling and steaming pans, and the fat bunches of herbs hanging to dry from the ceiling. People start to make their way outside and you follow them; the feasting is about to begin …

You are in Provence in summer, a place which has captured our collective imagination as being the epitome of the French countryside. The landscape and architecture of France vary hugely, from the half-timbered German-looking homes of Alsace to the stone-roofed houses set in the woods and hills of the Dordogne, but nowhere seems more French than Provence.

Food and the kitchen are at the heart of French country style, whatever the region. Food is an art form here, and the contemplation and consumption of it a national pastime. Even if the kitchen is small, more likely in the cities than in a château or converted farmhouse, it is always beautiful. Equipment is kept in peak condition. Rather than being hidden behind the cupboard doors of expensive kitchen units, it is often proudly displayed on open shelves, along with the pottery and china, ever ready to leap into action.

French kitchen equipment is among the best in the world (even if the French have rejected the idea of a kettle for boiling water), from the Le Creuset casseroles found in every English 'farmhouse' kitchen, to the gargantuan stainless-steel pans used by professional chefs everywhere. In the production of copperware, stainless-steel ware and pottery, the French are unrivalled. Swiss copper pans may be of equal quality, but they are made in only a fraction of the range of sizes available from France. When a recipe calls for a particular cooking utensil, most of us 'make do' with whatever comes to hand, whereas the French will use the exact type and size of pan specified.

The Provençal kitchen which fulfils our idea of the epitome of French country style is a spacious room – or it would be were it empty of furniture. For in addition to the equipment and furniture you would expect to find in a kitchen, including of course a large solid table, it has some special items such as the *panetière*. Known locally in Provence as a *panière*, this is a wall cupboard for storing freshly-baked bread. It is also an opportunity for the Provençal cabinetmaker to show off his skill at joinery, turning and carving, and generally to enjoy himself.

A *panetière* looks like a miniature pipe organ without a keyboard, on account of the many turned bars around the sides. The roof of the cupboard is crowned at the corners with top-knots known as *bobèches* or *chandelles*, sometimes sporting a whole regiment of these flourishes. The bottom has the four feet upon which all *panetières* once stood before someone thought of hanging theirs on a wall. The central door and horizontal panels above and below are vehicles for flamboyant carving. This might consist of simple curling lines, flower or heart shapes, or of elaborate urns, baskets, wheatsheafs, eglantine flowers and trailing vine leaves or myrtle.

Another important piece of furniture in the country kitchen and dining room is the *armoire*, a huge storage cupboard which was traditionally part of a bride's dowry. On these too craftsmen carved exuberant decoration which was often related to the event of a girl's marriage – sheaves of wheat or bunches of grapes, for example, refer-ring to her hoped-for fertility. An *armoire* has two doors closing onto a narrow central upright. Traditionally, each door has three panels with curving edges, and between these and the inside edge of each door, the finest examples have *ferrures*. These are narrow, lacy strips of iron or steel which are highly decorative, whilst protecting the doors from the effects of greasy fingers opening and closing them. Country furniture was inevitably made from wood which is plentiful locally, and in Provence that tradi-tionally meant walnut.

Observers have noticed that the prevailing culture of fine food and wine, bars and

A traditional Provençal print has been used here to cover a modern brass bed, its pillows and bolster. Tiny repeated prints comparable to these were especially popular in France in the 1800s. Napoleon is reputed to have bought lengths of the fabric for Josephine and the ladies of the court.

restaurants, and entertaining and eating away from home, has had a highly significant effect on the interior of French homes. With the emphasis on going out, the home has become hardly more than a base in which to sleep and keep your clothes.

In addition, the French attitude differs from that of other countries in that there is not the same mania for throwing out the furnishings and decorations of a few years ago in favour of a new look, be it ultra modern or, more likely in recent decades, flowers and frills or Victorian style. On the contrary, if furnishings still serve a practical purpose and are pleasing to the eye, why change them for change's sake? For example, fabrics such as Provençal prints and toile de Jouy are both immensely popular, even though, perhaps because, they each have a history going back centuries.

Toile is an instantly recognizable fabric which traditionally shows pastoral scenes from mythology and the classics (and, occasionally, historic events such as the first hot air balloon ascent and the American War of Independence) in a single colour on white or cream. Set up in 1770 in Jouy-en-Josas near Versailles, the first factory used copperplate printing to create the images on imported Indian calico. The fabrics were a success and in 1806 the founders (who were, ironically, German) set up their own cotton mill. Provençal prints are derived from *indiennes*, colourful Indian textiles imported into Marseilles in the seventeenth century. French versions were first manufactured there in 1656 and they were also made in Avignon.

The widespread popularity of these prints declined in the nineteenth century, and it looked as though the industry and tradition of these bright, printed floral and geometric fabrics, with their distinctive strong colours and repeating designs, might disappear completely.

However, during the second half of the twentieth century, traditional Provençal fabrics have undergone a renaissance, mainly thanks to one man. Charles Deméry took over a fabric printing company in 1938 and rescued an astonishing collection of 40,000 wooden printing blocks. These formed the basis of the designs on fabrics sold by the company Souleiado ever since. After the war years this company upgraded production, converting to synthetic dyes and large-scale roller printing methods, and the popularity of the fabrics rose once again. Today the name Souleiado is world-famous, and has become synonymous with Provençal patterns and colours. Such popularity can only have helped the few other small companies that also produce traditional Provençal prints. Souleiado fabrics, meanwhile, are available in many countries outside France, and the company also produces a large catalogue of its designs which is available by mail order.

Another consideration affecting the look of French homes is the fact that among owners of old homes in particular, DIY has never been perceived as a jolly weekend activity involving the whole family, as it is elsewhere. If you need something done, you hire a professional who knows what he or she is about and will do a job that will last.

This beautiful iron table was found in the cellar when the current owners moved into their 1810 house near Moulins, right in the heart of France. The chair is early twentieth century; the cloth is a magnificent 'table carpet', a thickly woven fabric, with the vibrant colours and flamboyant design of the style of Napoleon III.

In recent decades there has been some increased interest in interior decoration in France. The President's palace, L'Elysée, is now regularly redecorated to create a showcase for the best of French decoration and design. But in the meantime, the average French home has escaped the frills and fuss of some styles of decoration. The result is a fresh, simple look based on the lines of the building itself and the function of the objects within, which themselves have a direct, graphic quality which makes them eminently desirable.

Since the beginning of the twentieth century, a large shift in population has taken place in France, and this too has had an effect on French interiors. In 1900 as much as half the population lived in the country. Today that number has dropped to well below ten per cent. This migration to the cities has resulted in large numbers of agricultural buildings and country houses coming onto the market. The new owners are city people or foreigners acquiring a holiday home; they are people such as artists and craftsmen who do not need to be in the city for their work; they are businesspeople who can do most of their work from home with the aid of computers, telecommunications and other modern technology; or they are wealthy people 'getting away from the smog', leaving behind the dirt and stress of their former urban existence. Whoever they are, they are not the traditional peasant in blue cotton overalls, his *bleu de travail*, with his wife swathed in black.

The newcomers have brought with them a dash of elegance and sophistication which blends well with their hearty admiration for all things French and for the ways of the countryside into which they have moved. The wealthier locals have themselves become more sophisticated, meanwhile, adopting the best of modern ways. One of the houses photographed for this book is a traditional *mas* (farmhouse) in the Camargue – complete with fax machine.

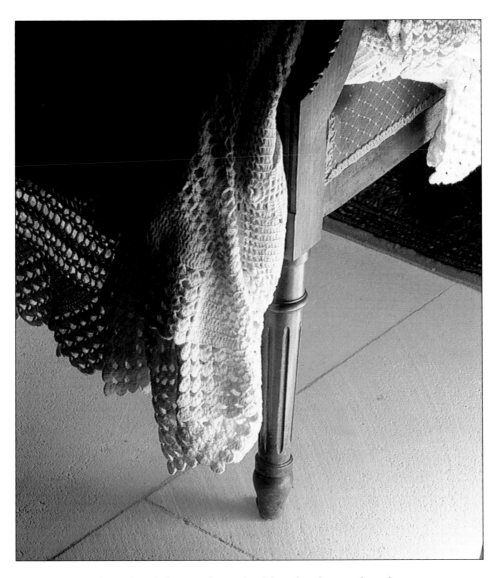

Light shining through the pattern in a crocheted throw draped over an elegant banquette.

This new French style, a sort of *style haut paysan*, exists alongside a country style that derives from France's proud history of centuries of interior decoration in the grand manner. The impetus and money for such enterprise came from royalty and the top echelons of noble and wealthy society, and examples can be seen today in the many châteaux open to the public. While the fruits of this tradition, its furniture and objets, are sought after across the world, at home in France it continues, albeit generally on a more modest scale.

In the mid-1970s, I visited a home with echoes of this tradition, whose quietly opulent elegance would have been alarming had it not been so comfortable and seductive. The house, in a small town in the Loire valley, was stone-built and of a comfortable size rather than enormous, with four bedrooms. Its proportions were not imposing, but its decoration seemed to me to be as grand, in parts, as any stately home I had ever visited as a tourist.

The most fascinating room was the study or library, in which the family sat when they wished to be cosy. Never had I seen so much rich, vibrant pattern in one room. The sofas and chairs were upright and tapering, quite unlike the large, squashily embracing sofas found in an English country house. They were all covered with the same bold fabric of traditional design, showing thick ropes of intertwined rich red and pink flowers and green foliage against a white background.

But the thing that bowled you over was the fact that the *walls* were covered with this fabric too. How was it done? Enquiries revealed that the fabric was nailed to thin battens of wood which were in turn fixed to the walls. But I never saw a single tell-tale nail or screw, the fabric was as smooth as ice, without a single gather or tuck, and all the lines of the pattern were straight. It was a marvel of decorating at which I gazed in awe. My hosts were amused by this strange child's interest.

One wall of this room was occupied by a huge bookcase, the type of large piece of furniture which dominates so many French country living rooms. Its upper doors were glazed so that one could see the collection housed within. This included some leather-bound books with gold lettering on their spines. Far more interesting, however, were the objects lying in front of the books – arranged there, one might say, had their 'arrangement' not appeared so entirely artless, in the same way that the clothes and appearance of a French man or woman can seem so effortlessly elegant. No other country has such a reputation for this gift.

In the bookcase, ivory opera glasses, tiny kid gloves, elaborate silver and enamel boxes, a fountain pen, small bronze animals, an exquisite linen and lace handkerchief embroidered with the letter 'E', miniature portrait paintings of forebears, babies' teething rings and christening mugs ... so many small treasures of great age and beauty were here massed together so nonchalantly.

This net curtain is of a type known as 'château curtains', and is made from a hand-embroidered fine cotton voile. The draped curtain is actually a nineteenth-century linen sheet with a seam along the middle, indicating that it was domestically made on a small loom.

Other rooms in a French country house can seem surprisingly spartan by contrast with the warmth and elegance of living rooms and bedrooms. Bathrooms are often purely utilitarian, unfitted and plain white, decorated from floor to ceiling with gleaming

One curving end of a traditional nineteenth-century French 'lit bateau', literally 'boat bed'. The quilt was found in a Lyon fleamarket.

white tiles, and without any apparent concession to comfort. Baths and basins are large and heavy, massive reminders of a previous age.

One of the things which surprised me on my first visit to France was a detail which in retrospect seems small and rather charming. There were no chests of drawers. Not in my bedroom; nor, apparently, in any other room in the house. I had been shown a wardrobe with some hanging space above a shelf where, I was told, I could put my 'linen'. This misunderstanding was soon sorted out; by 'linen' I was not meant to understand sheets and pillowcases (which of course I had not brought with me) but any clothes which didn't hang up, such as underwear, and the wardrobe was intended to house all one's clothes.

The typical French country bedroom is a charming place, a fusion of the simple and the sophisticated. The wooden floor is polished and bare, except perhaps for a handsome rug. The window is likely to possess a traditional pair of tall, overlapping casements, secured with a twist-action long-bolt fastening and veiled with a simple net curtain. The bed may be narrow and not especially comfortable, but it will probably have a prettily carved head and foot.

The wardrobe will often take up a large part of the remaining space and in the corner there may be a simple handbasin with old chrome taps. This will sometimes be hidden from the rest of the room by an elegant little fabric-covered folding screen. The extreme fastidiousness of such an arrangement may seem startling at first, but it makes sense. After all, who enjoys looking at half-empty bottles and jars and half-squeezed tubes of toothpaste?

The strangest room in an old-fashioned French country house, however, is likely to be the lavatory. I once visited a house where this was a narrow, dark room with a small window at the opposite end from the door. Just below the window was an edifice

This kitchen chair and the traditional Provençal fabric covering the cushion were picked up by the owners in their local market.

which resembled a throne. A polished wooden bench filled the entire width of the room and had a broad step on which one climbed to reach the seat. This was a smooth round hole carved in the bench and covered with a lid. To flush the lavatory, you reached into a small indentation near the seat and lifted a porcelain knob which activated a deafening gush of water. Many old country houses are still more likely to rely on a cesspit rather than mains sewerage.

One of the greatest fans of French style in all its forms is the British designer Terence Conran, who once summed up his feelings with the words: 'All the best things come from France.' In the introduction to his book *Terence Conran's France* he describes the enormous impression made upon him by his first visit to the country, in 1952. 'I took in the excitement, colour and graphic abundance of the street markets, the beauty of shabby exterior decay on rural buildings, the light and texture of the countryside, and the fresh, functional design of everything from advertising typography to enamelled coffee pots ... '

His love of all things French has been infectious: during his years as a retailer with the Habitat and Conran shops in Britain, continental Europe, the USA and Japan, he has introduced a whole generation of people to the joys of owning and using well-designed French kitchenware. He popularized such objects as the cafetière and the wooden salad bowl, without which no contemporary home is complete today, but which were almost unheard of outside continental Europe before the first Habitat shop opened in May 1964 in the Fulham Road in London. Needless to say, Terence Conran has a house in the French countryside where he spends part of the year. Would that every francophile amongst us could do the same! If we could, however, there would barely be a Frenchman left in the countryside to perpetuate the magnificent charm and warmth of true French country style.

DOORS

IN A FRENCH COUNTRY HOUSE, THE CRAFTS-
MANSHIP DISPLAYED IN THE DESIGN OF IRON-
WORK SUCH AS DOOR FITTINGS IS LIKELY TO BE
SUPERB; AND THE STYLE AND FINISH OF THE
DOORS THEMSELVES WILL GIVE YOU A CLUE AS
TO WHAT LIES WITHIN...

A magnificent rim latch and lock with curlicue handle,
original to the kitchen door which it fastens in a mid-
eighteenth-century bastide *in Provence.*

This solid, matt-painted, dusty-blue plank door complete with a window hatch belongs to a farm cottage in Brittany.

An old straw boater hangs from one of two decorative hooks on the back of a blue-painted door in a house in Les Landes.

One of two solid oak front doors opening into a traditional Provençal bastide. The ironwork on the door is substantial and magnificent: knob, knocker, fingerplate and huge nails studding the lower part all illustrate the skill and artistry of local ferronniers or blacksmiths.

The doorknob on the front door (left) is a delightful illustration of the blacksmith's art. The knob is constructed from a whorl of squared iron strands, each of which has been twisted. The strands come together behind a solid blob of iron.

Another delightful piece of ironwork, this time a bedroom door handle upstairs in the Provençal bastide.

A pretty brass bedroom door-bolt which, in spite of its six screws attaching it to the door, is hardly robust.

*A magnificent brass bedroom window-catch. This bedroom belonged to the lady of
the house, so the fittings are especially fine.*

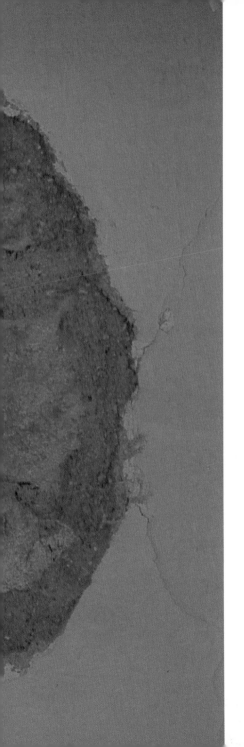

FLOORS, STAIRS & WINDOWS

FRANCE HAS GIVEN ITS NAME TO THE GENER-
OUS AND PRACTICAL, FULL-LENGTH OPENING
'FRENCH WINDOW', FOUND THE WORLD OVER.
NO WONDER WINDOWS IN FRENCH COUNTRY
HOUSES ARE SO DELECTABLE, AS ARE
SIMPLE FLOORS AND STAIRCASES.

*This tiny unglazed window has recently been punched
through a wall to ventilate a new bathroom. It reveals
the thickness of the wall, which helps keep the old mill
warm in winter and cool in summer.*

*Old terracotta floor tiles in Provence. The lozenge shaped ones are, predictably, more unusual than the plain
squares. Tiles and stone floors help to keep houses cool in the terrific heat of summer.*

These ancient chestnut floorboards taper because they were cut from whole trees. This mill is still surrounded by chestnut groves of the type from which the wood, naturally impervious to beetles, has been cut for centuries to make almost everything found locally.

———————

This type of straight-up, rustic staircase with no banister rail is known as an
échelle de meunier, *a 'miller's ladder', and in this case that was literally so, since*
the stairs lead to the former granary in an old mill. The banisters visible at the top
were made from a manger found in the cattle shed on the ground floor of the house.

A staircase constructed from stone,
wood, tiles and iron, the newel (or
bottom post) revealing once again
the Provençal craftsman's skill with
wrought iron.

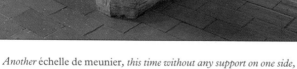

Another échelle de meunier, *this time without any support on one side,
making it especially precarious, even for a sober adult.*

*The colours used on the woodwork and exterior of Provençal houses are vivid and
fresh when applied, but quickly and beautifully fade in the blazing summer sun.*

*These enamel jugs, with their pretty arrangement of dried grasses, stand in an
original stone sink beneath a newer window in the kitchen of a centuries-old mill in
south-west France.*

*A particularly pretty window fastening. When the handle is lifted from the catch,
the left-hand casement can be opened slightly to allow air in. The handle may then
be dropped to secure the window from swinging further open.*

A blue-painted iron window catch of particularly elegant design incorporating star shapes, with a pretty brass knob.

PATTERN
& COLOUR

Patterned French fabrics, such as traditional Provençal prints with their
luscious colours and designs, are among
the most coveted in the world, and the
French use of pattern is among the
boldest.

*A handsome mid-nineteenth-century carved and
painted wooden bed was upholstered with this fabric in
the 1940s; the pattern complements the hand-blocked
wallpaper which is original to this early nineteenth-
century house.*

White tiles with a fresh blue and yellow pattern line this bathroom; the chrome towel rail is typical of this house which has one by every basin.

Dappled light increases the range of colours on an old Spanish cupboard in the summer dining room of a house near Bordeaux. The room is open to the elements on two sides.

Detail of a magnificent table 'carpet'.

The traditional fabrics of Provence are based on Indian prints imported into France in the seventeenth century and are still produced by the company Souleiado, using modern techniques. This fabric is No. 1078-05 (Petite fleur des champs) *from* La Collection Traditionelle, *with border No. 1459-01* (La Pitchune).

Another ravishing Souleiado fabric in a mas *in the Camargue, this time No. 1402-00, called* La Pompadour, *with a magnificent wide border No. 1405-0* (Le grand rose). *Souleiado fabrics are available outside France .*

Wallpaper decorated with a pattern in the grand style, in the salon of a house in the Loire. The function of the chair rail is to protect the lower paper from damage by chair backs and feet.

A close-up view of a remarkable piece of craftsmanship, a huge bedcover made by the owner's grandmother in 1910. The white cotton crocheted cover has been made to a particular design which is a Provençal speciality.

KITCHENS

The contemplation, preparation and consumption of fresh food is a serious national pastime in France. The kitchen therefore tends to be the focus of the home, especially in the country, and is filled with delicious sights and smells.

A collection of enamelware, including a set of six kitchen storage jars found at a summer brocante *fair. In France, only objects that are a hundred years old or more count as antique; the rest are know as '*brocante*', roughly translatable as 'high class junk'.*

A deliciously welcoming scene in the home of writer Peter Mayle near Menerbes in the Luberon district of Provence.
The elegant shelves on the back wall are antique and were once a baker's display.

The kitchen is the heart of the house in many French country homes such as this one, where assorted chairs, including a rush-seated child's high chair, are gathered around a table covered with patterned cloth.

A shallow eighteenth-century kitchen sink made from a type of granite found in north-eastern France and local to this house.

The contemplation and consumption of food are national pastimes in France, with good reason. This corner of a French kitchen is crammed with utensils and, most important, vegetables, bread and cheese.

The hatch of a charbonnière, *a sort of mobile coal bunker. This one is kept close to the range that it feeds (right) but can be wheeled away on its castors to be refilled.*

An extraordinary enamelled cast-iron range in a farmhouse in the Loire. It was made in about 1920 and is typical of the region – there were several manufacturers in St Etienne where there was a tradition of coal mining and iron foundry. Fired by solid fuel – either wood or coal – it is still in use today.

A dresser supporting fruity objects is surrounded by paintings of fruit by the owners of the house.

A beautiful nineteenth-century set of hooks in wirework hangs below an advertisement board promoting coffee. Whole shops were once boarded up when the owner died, because of France's complicated inheritance laws, so there is often plenty of charming ephemera like this to be found in provincial flea markets.

An early twentieth-century enamelled iron splashback on which to hang ladles and other kitchen utensils. The tray at the bottom catches any drips. Splashbacks were made with many different patterns and colours but were mostly of the same size and design. Next to it hangs a salt box.

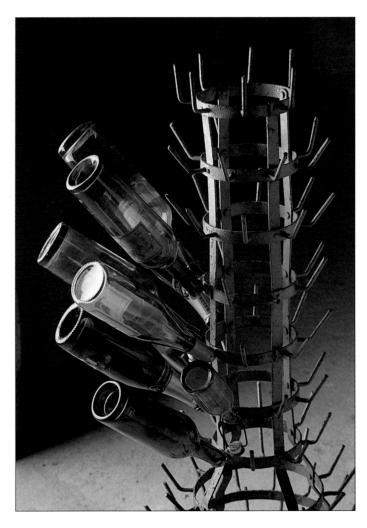

A painted metal bottle-rack for drying washed bottles. These are still found in use in French country homes and were once also used in restaurants. Glass bottles were reused because they were more valuable than the local wine kept in them – a case of recycling from economic necessity.

Local olive oil is found alongside imported Italian oil and dried herbs from the garden on a windowsill in a Provençal kitchen. The flavour and scent of oil, herbs and garlic, with vegetables such as aubergines and peppers in season, is typical of the region's cookery.

LIVING
ROOMS

OUTSIDE THE KITCHEN, OTHER COUNTRY LIV-

ING ROOMS TEND TO BE BOLDLY DECORATED

OR FURNISHED, WITH MAGNIFICENT FURNI-

TURE LIKE THE TRADITIONAL ARMOIRE AND

PANETIÈRE.

A magnificent example of a panetière, *the typically Provençal wall-hung cupboard in which bread is stored to keep it fresh. Carvings on the front panels show flowers, game and wheatsheaves.*

The owner of this house was studying interior design when she decorated the rooms using richly-coloured paints on all of the woodwork. She also removed many panels of infill between the timber supports, introducing light and air into a previously gloomy house.

A close-up of the armoire (seen left) showing in detail the exuberance of the carving down the middle, and the ferrures which help to protect the doors of the cupboard from being marked by fingerprints.

A splendid armoire in the dining room of a house in the Camargue. Storage cupboards such as this were often part of a bride's dowry. This has the typical three panels on each door with especially fine carving across the top and down the middle, and fine ferrures (metal strips) on the doors.

*An early nineteenth-century inlaid floor in front of a contemporary fireplace in a
country house near Moulins.*

*This enamelled stove is in the same house as the enamelled kitchen range on
page 128 and was made around the same time, in the 1920s.*

The fireplace in the living room of a thousand-year-old mill in the Aveyron area of south-west France. Locals can still remember a time when they gathered around the fire, drinking, singing and gossiping while their grain was ground. When the owners bought the long-abandoned mill five years ago the cauldron over the fire was their only source of hot water.

The overmantel of the fireplace in a Breton farm cottage, edged with a pretty Christmassy baldaquin or canopy, and used to store coffee bowls, soup plates, glasses, bottles and a paraffin lamp.

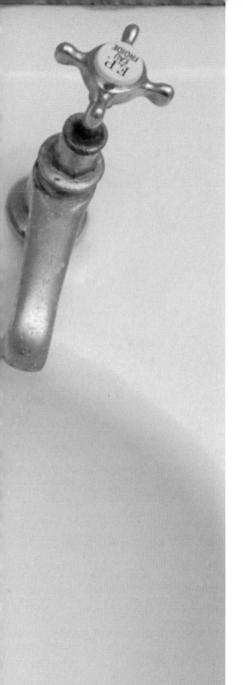

BEDROOMS

&

BATHROOMS

IN A FRENCH COUNTRY BEDROOM, THE FUR-

NISHINGS ARE LIKELY TO BE SIMPLE BUT

ELEGANT; THE BATHROOMS MAY BE UTILI-

TARIAN BUT MAGNIFICENT, WITH ANTIQUE

CHINA AND FITTINGS.

An excellent example of a solid plain white basin with
old chrome taps.

A modern brass bed covered with a bedspread made from an old piece of fabric decorated with a traditional Provençal print. This is one of the bedrooms in a Provençal bastide which the owners let on a bed-and-breakfast basis.

A room known as the 'Queen's Bedroom' in a mas *in the Camargue. The collection of watches and religious artefacts belonged to the owner's great-grandmother.*

Box beds in a restored farm cottage in Brittany. This bed and the one opposite are alongside each other on one wall of the cottage's only room, used for eating, cooking, sleeping and living in.

146

In beds like these, a huge straw mattress, perhaps 60 cm (2 ft) thick, would have been topped with a large 'duvet' filled with oat chaff, or feathers if you could afford them.

A huge iron bath with magnificent feet and plumbing; of the four taps, the middle two are hot and cold, the bottom operates the bath tap and the top the shower.

A bathroom that is utilitarian but majestic in scale, with a voluptuous double basin, vast bath, handsome radiator and elegant chrome fittings. The basin was made by Porcher, a French company still in production.

Two single basins joined to make a 'double' with a neat centre panel. Sadly the original taps have been replaced with less than elegant modern mixer taps.

This charming, nineteenth-century handbasin was reclaimed from another building and installed in the recently restored ancient mill in the Aveyron.

A handsome nineteenth-century cast-iron bathroom radiator with sinuous scrolled decorations.

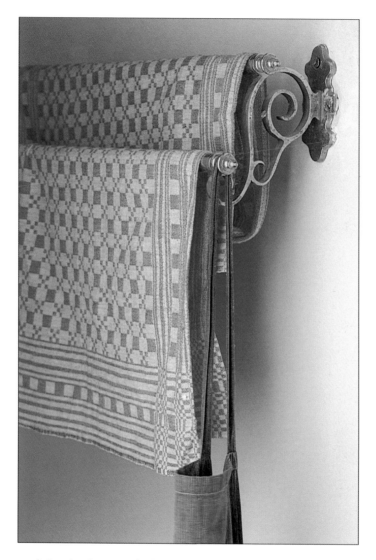

A charming chrome towel rail in the nineteenth-century house near Moulins.

A flimsy cupboard door, with cut-out star or flower shapes for decoration, has been transformed into the door of a room by having a strip of wood added to its top and bottom. This door was bought from the famous gypsies of Ronda, who organize architectural reclamation as well as making new traditional furniture from pine.

CASA
Southern Spanish Style

THE STYLE OF SOUTHERN SPAIN IS AS DISTINCTIVE AS THE MAGNIFICENT FESTIVAL regalia of a matador – no-one could possibly mistake it for anything else. And, like the matador's costume, it has its origins in traditions formed in centuries past. If the north of Spain, and the city of Barcelona in particular, is perceived as being the powerhouse of all things modern in art, design, architecture and interiors, so the south, and Andalucia in particular, is keeper of a large part of Spain's decorative past.

Just the word 'Andalucia' conjures up poetic images which speak of the Moors, southern Spain's Arab inhabitants for hundreds of years. The influence of their philosophy concerning buildings and gardens is felt even today. The play of brilliant sunlight on the slender columns of pavilions in the exquisite Alhambra Palace in Granada, striped horseshoe arches in the mosque of Cordoba, geometric patterns on panels of gleaming coloured tiles, inner paved courtyards, palm trees, still pools of water and above all, the sound of fountains playing: these are among the elements which, together, give southern Spanish style its historical resonance.

The influence of the Moors is ingrained in the imagination of Andalucians, as Gerald Brennan, an Englishman who went to live in a remote part of Andalucia immediately after the First World War, soon discovered. In his charming book *South of*

155

Granada, which describes his years in Yegen, he wrote, 'When I first arrived in the village and spoke of the war in which I had been taking part, many people supposed I had been fighting the Moors.'

Southern Spain's early history is colourful and dramatic. Successive invasions by Phoenicians, Greeks, Celts and Carthaginians gave way in the first century BC to settlement by the Romans, who founded the city of Cordoba, later famous for its mosque and the flowering of Islamic scholarship. Phoenicians are supposed to have given Spain her name, from their word for rabbit, 'sapan'(at the time Spain was heavily wooded and was overrun with rabbits). Visigoths subsequently conquered the Iberian peninsula in the fifth century.

Each race of settlers brought with them creative skills and styles, some of which became absorbed into the indigenous culture. The Celts and Visigoths, for example, were superb ironsmiths who made the most of Spain's great metal deposits. They introduced skills developed to ever greater heights by fifteenth- and sixteenth-century artists and artisans and still venerated in modern times by people of taste. Metal deposits are still mined at the site of ancient excavations in western Andalucia, making them the oldest mines in the world.

The two types of metalwork you are most likely to see in Spain today are the locks, studs and decorative straps on old wooden chests and doors, and *rejas.* The latter are the heavy and often elaborately wrought old iron grilles covering the street-facing windows of houses in cities, towns and villages. These served the purpose not only of keeping out brigands and other intruders but also of protecting your unmarried daughters within. As late as the early twentieth century, a well-brought-up young woman in Seville or Granada only ever saw her *novio,* or boyfriend, through this grille (or from an upstairs balcony) until they were formally betrothed.

Dappled sunlight falls on the reja *of an old door in a village near Seville.*

The great period of Moorish culture in Andalucia lasted from early in the eighth century, when the Moors invaded and conquered the Visigoth kingdom, until January 1492, when the 'Catholic Monarchs', Isabella and Ferdinand, recaptured Granada. The Moors inevitably brought a great influx of Islamic culture, developed in the near east and incorporating influences which included the Byzantine and Roman. This met and absorbed many deep-rooted indigenous skills and styles, to emerge with a strong, energetic, confident, individual and almost fully formed identity of its own. Above all, though it had much in common with Islamic styles in other countries, it was distinctively Iberian.

The Spanishness that characterizes every period of Spain's artistic heritage is due in part to the geography of the Iberian peninsula, which is almost a huge island, joined to the rest of Europe by a stretch of unfriendly Pyrenean mountains three hundred miles (roughly five hundred kilometres) wide. In the south, it stretches to within nine miles (about fifteen kilometres) of Africa. The only neighbouring country with which it shares the peninsula is Portugal, a fraction of its size.

One example of the sort of marriage behind what we think of as Moorish style is the traditional layout of a Moorish home, which in fact combined Christian, Roman and Islamic ideas in a model of perfection. In Islam, the sky framed by the perimeter of your courtyard is your own little piece of heaven. The principles of garden design which the Moors introduced were based on rhythm and geometry, encapsulated in an enclosed garden or courtyard with pillared porticoes and pavilions. Paradise is portrayed as a garden in Islam, as it is in other religions, including Christianity with its Garden of Eden. Meanwhile the plan of the house, with rooms opening onto the central courtyard, is inherited from the Romans.

The importance of having a palm tree in your courtyard (as opposed to any other tree) goes back to a Moorish caliph, founder of the great mosque of Cordoba and of the Umaiyad dynasty of rulers. He is said to have planted one of the first date palms in Spain to remind himself of Syria, his homeland. Among other things he was a poet, and described himself as an 'immigrant stranger', akin to his lonely palm. Later in the same caliphate, which lasted for three centuries, there are believed to have been over fifty thousand verdant gardens in Cordoba, varying in size but most of them organized around the all-important palm tree.

The Koran describes paradise as 'a garden flowing with streams'. When Granada became the capital of the Moorish territories, the Darro river was diverted, by means of a feat of engineering, from the valley below to the top of the mountain, where the Alhambra Palace now stands. Water makes a vital and magical contribution to the Alhambra's spellbinding atmosphere. In the Court of Myrtles it is perfectly still, lying in a long and narrow rectangular pool which reflects the shrubs and buildings alongside; in the Court of Lions it is constantly moving, shimmering in the basin and burbling in the fountain and the jets that fall from the lions' mouths.

In architecture, the Moorish detail which is most often to be found in Andalucian homes today is the horseshoe arch. This juts out slightly where the arch meets the vertical sides of the archway opening. The most spectacular example of the use of arches in Andalucian architecture is the mosque at Cordoba. Here, hundreds of pillars support striped arches, with yet more arches rising up above the first tier. The effect is enthralling, the geometry and repetition of lines and arcs managing to be restful and thrilling at the same time. The well-known travel writer H.V. Morton visited Spain in the 1950s and described his impression of the mosque in *A Stranger in Spain*:

The entrance to the renovated olive press attached to an old senorial house and chapel near Seville. Oil is made in presses in the village once again.

> In the morning I went to the mosque of Cordoba, with no intention of al-
> lowing myself to be carried away by enthusiasm, but in two minutes I was
> vanquished. Of all the buildings of the Islamic world this is to me the most
> fantastic ... It reminds me of an immense forest full of zebras. The striped
> red and white arches stretch away in innumerable vistas, and whichever way
> you look you see the same view. It is like a trick with mirrors, yet the feeling
> it roused in me was one of delight ... What ought to have been a failure was a
> brilliant success.

The furnishing of southern Spanish houses can appear sparse. There is no great amount of old or antique furniture available to anyone decorating a home. Spain does not have the same tradition of fine furniture as is found in some other parts of Europe. Even in grand houses pieces tend to be robust and often heavily carved. In the whole country, there have been few great designers and craftsmen whose names stand out in the history of furniture, as do Chippendale and Sheraton in England, for example. Added to which, quantities of old furniture are thought to have been burnt as fuel during the desperate years of the Civil War.

Those pieces which do exist in Andalucia are fairly rough and ready. They mostly consist of folding chairs and folding x-shaped stools, their forms derived from Visigoth and Moorish pieces which folded to make them easily transportable. Other items which can be found are traditional chests and occasional *bargueños* (table-top writing desks), or simple peasant furniture.

Some modern pine tables and chairs are made in the style of traditional peasant originals, the latter usually having rush seating. The Muños family, based in Ronda, is famous in contemporary Andalucia for making a thriving business out of manufacturing such furniture. A large family of gypsies with connections across the entire country, the Muñoses also have a firm grip on the architectural reclamation business. They can take the credit for having made a worthwhile industry out of saving great numbers of doors, *rejas* and other architectural antiques, in a country where enthusiasm for old buildings is confined to an enlightened élite.

One of the most extraordinary and distinctive pieces of furniture found in Andalucia is a type of round table called a *mesa camilla*. This has two tiers: the upper one at normal height serves as a table at which you sit; the lower one has a metal bucket set in the middle, in which burning charcoal is placed for heating. Houses in southern Spain do not have heating systems, the only heat coming from fireplaces and cookers. The *mesa camilla* offers a cosy place to sit on cool evenings and in winter. Gerald Brennan describes its use in *South from Granada*:

> This classic piece of furniture and the domestic rites accompanying it demand some explanation. Imagine then a circular deal table with a brazier of wood ash or charcoal set under it. Drape over it a red-flannel tablecloth that reaches on every side to the ground, and let three, four or six persons sit around it with the skirts of this tablecloth, which are split into sections, tucked about them. Let them have short coats or shawls thrown lightly over their backs and let their faces be leaning towards one another – either deep in a game of cards, or sewing, or else perfectly still and motionless, merely rippling the silence from time to time by some placid observation. Then you will have a picture of what family life is like during one half of the year in every town and village of this country.

Colours in Andalucian homes are often rich and strong, offset by brilliant white walls and blinding sunlight, or they are beautifully faded, mellow versions of their former selves, bleached by the sun. Reds, oranges, ochres, greens ... the tones reflect the colours of the landscape, plants and flowers of the region. In the rest of Spain blue is not generally a popular colour because it is perceived as cool, even chilly, and because the dye was once rare and too costly to use. In Andalucia, however, the heat and brilliant sun counteract its coolness and blue is used to great effect.

Brilliant sunlight falling on a charmingly elaborate bell at the front gate of a house in Andalucia casts an intriguing pattern on the whitewashed wall behind.

Terracotta floors are used extensively and give warmth of colour to any room. They vary in tone depending on their age and, if they are new, on the method used to seal them. After being laid with a cement mortar, the tiles or thin bricks are cleaned with an astringent agent such as industrial vinegar. Then they are sealed, either with a modern silicone-based sealant, which does not darken the floor greatly, or with the more traditional linseed oil, which darkens and enriches the colour. Other possible sealants include paraffin and even petrol.

A pair of small wooden stools with inlaid seats, standing on a terracotta tiled floor.

Typical Andalucian style, however, gives little space to textiles. Windows are small and generally have shutters rather than curtains. And furniture is usually wooden, though upholstered furniture and loose covers which would not look out of place in an English drawing room can be found in the homes of both foreigners and the more eclectic Spaniards. Another reason for the lack of fabrics is the climate. The strong sunlight and humidity is unkind to cloth, shortening its life considerably. Such textiles as there are tend to be cotton, linen and, occasionally, wool. Linen flax was traditionally grown in Galicia, but Franco's policies in the 1960s brought this to an end and today it is imported.

Much of the colour in a southern Spanish interior comes from ceramics – pottery and tiles. There is a long and rich history of ceramics in Spain. The Arabs are believed to have introduced refined oriental techniques, establishing potteries near Granada and Malaga. Here both tiles and ceramic vessels were made with metal lustre decoration – a technique which later went out of fashion and was lost, to be rediscovered in northern Europe in the nineteenth century.

Tiles are cool, practical and their glazed surfaces reflect light. Moorish architecture made extensive use of tiles for decoration, indoors and out, on every imaginable surface. Patterns included angular Cufic, and later flowing Cursive script for quotations from the Koran. Other semi-abstract decoration used plant forms, flowers, arabesques and geometric stars in patterns of such intricacy and variety that they created a feast for the eye.

Modern Spanish pottery varies greatly in design quality, the most attractive usually being the least pretentious. Simple, bold shapes and colourful, flowing decoration is the most pleasing and is found on jugs and mugs, plates, bowls and dishes of every shape and size. Decoration on the best modern tiles has a similarly unrestrained look and frequently uses star shapes and other motifs derived from Moorish designs. Another traditional type of ceramic which inspires modern tile makers is majolica ware, in which colourful pictures were painted onto tiles with green, blue and ochre-yellow glazes. This technique was introduced into Seville from Italy around 1500 by Francisco Niculoso. Original tiles from Moorish times and the Renaissance are very rare but not unheard-of in contemporary homes.

One person who was lucky enough to come across a cache of antique tiles is antique dealer Malcolm Davidson, who lives near Cadiz. Found in a barn, the tiles were laid out on the floor to be matched up before the major part was sold; fortunately there were sufficient left-over individual and small sets of tiles for the Davidsons and a neighbour to use in the construction of fireplaces. The tiles are believed originally to have decorated a palace in Seville or Cordoba, where they would have been used between the wooden beams to line a ceiling.

One of the great paradoxes of southern Spanish style is the huge gulf between the richness of Andalucian cultural heritage and common contemporary attitudes to anything antique. It is as great as the gulf in time between the Moors and modern Spain. Among most ordinary Spaniards (not including aristocrats, families with old money, the best designers and some artists and other people of taste) attitudes towards old buildings and their renovation, and indeed old things in general, vary little. They would rather have everything new: new clothes, new furniture, new houses.

A naturalized Spaniard, formerly an interior designer in England, points out:

> Spain is twenty years behind in many things, because of the years of repression caused by the Civil War in the 1930s and then the dictatorship of General Franco. Spaniards are catching up, but they still love everything new and plastic and they chuck out old things. I have found magnificent doors on skips. The movement to renovate old buildings is very new amongst ordinary people.

A detail of the fireplace on page 200 (left), showing close up the colour and delightfully lively decoration of the antique tiles with which it is inlaid.

Wicker baskets, old glass flagons and jars of local olives on a shelf above the cooker in the kitchen of an old house in Andalucia.

Added to this, the climate in Andalucia can be brutal. Sometimes after five summer months without rain you can hardly move or breath outdoors – and buildings, often badly built in the first place, suffer in the extremes. Eventually they rot or crumble and are pulled down. This lack of tenderness in the climate and in so many aspects of Andalucia applies to the treatment of old buildings. Much of the landscape and vegetation, the character of the people, even Flamenco singing and dancing, is harsh and uncompromising. Sacheverell Sitwell referred to this aspect of the country in 1961 when he wrote, 'No land in Europe, probably no other land in the civilized world, has so violent a personality, so strong a flavour, as that of Spain.'

Happily, those who do appreciate them find that the skills needed to restore, convert and extend their homes still exist among tradesmen and artisans. Building materials such as terracotta roof and floor tiles are still made in Andalucia, old windows and doors can be bought from the gypsies of Ronda as can new furniture based on old designs. Tiles and ceramics are plentiful. Using all these elements, the most splendid southern Spanish interiors bring together the old and the new, embracing Andalucia's magnificent heritage with contemporary vigour.

HALLS
& STAIRS

HALLWAYS OF ANDALUCIAN HOUSES DRAW
YOU FROM THE OUTDOOR HEAT AND DUST,
THROUGH A HEAVILY DEFENSIVE WOODEN
DOOR BRAZENED WITH IRON STUDS AND
STRAPS, INTO A COOL, TILED INTERIOR. TILED
AND PAINTED STAIRWAYS LEAD YOU FURTHER
AWAY FROM THE SUN. PLANTS AND TREES
FLOURISH HERE, SHELTERED FROM THE
BLISTERING BRIGHTNESS.

*This front door of a casita is probably a hundred years
old. The door-within-a-door is designed to let in a little
light and obviate the need for a window. The tiled floor
can be glimpsed within - square terracotta tiles with
small glazed, coloured inserts.*

171

*Massive old chestnut doors, original to this Andalucian house, open into the hall.
The lefthand door has a small hatch which opens to let in light and air when the doors are
closed against the sun's heat. Called a* postigo, *this one has its original lock. Locally-
made terracotta tiles cover the floor.*

The hall-cum-living room of artist Maria Foixa's home, with stairs leading to the next half-floor. The house, converted from storehouses belonging to the Archbishop of Seville, has a number of different levels. The walls of this room have been painted with ochre pigments and the stairs are lined below with antique tiles.

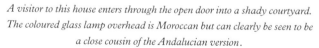

A visitor to this house enters through the open door into a shady courtyard. The coloured glass lamp overhead is Moroccan but can clearly be seen to be a close cousin of the Andalucian version.

*A solid modern staircase with painted plaster sides and brightly painted risers
leads to bedrooms and a living room. Space underneath the stairs has been cleverly used to
provide storage for firewood.*

*An elegant modern staircase built of bricks, plastered and painted ochre.
The treads have been laid with tiles and the stark, sinuous contours of the staircase are
softened with a mass of plants.*

Detail of an old and pretty wrought-iron reja, *or window grille, retained for security on a window facing the street. Modern* rejas *do not have the same elegance and charm, being made in general from sheet metal.*

An exquisite mid-nineteenth-century wrought-iron gateway rescued from a demolished palace by reclamation dealers. The owner of this house fell in love with it, bought it, and then had to build a wall to accommodate it.

DOORS &
WINDOWS

Doors and windows in the houses of
southern Spain have a special charm.
Whether they are bold and massive
or small and delicate, they are always
interesting. Sometimes there is a door
within a door, or a window within a
window, or they are enlivened by carving
or a pretty *REJA* (window grille).

A typical window within a door, the small hatch
allowing a little light and air to enter when the massive
studded front door is closed against intruders and
the searing heat.

A small corner cupboard, installed when the house was converted from farm outbuildings about twenty years ago. Lattice work is frequently used for Andalucian cupboard doors, to allow some air to circulate in the hot climate. The pretty pottery lamp is Portuguese.

The front door of a house near Seville, parts of which are five hundred years old. The chandelier is modern, made locally and available in the Reina Carlotta shop in the village of Cazalla de la sierra near Seville, and by mail order.

A hall cupboard painted white and aubergine. The hinges are a typical Andalucian design.

A beautiful pair of carved wooden doors in Maria Foixa's sitting room
(see also pages 200 and 208).

A splendid green-painted front door with iron studs and a decorative circular air vent. You turn a small handle inside to open and close the vent, according to the weather.

A very old wooden window (top) has recently had a smaller window made within one pane. This allows the owner to air the room without opening the whole window. The sill is covered with modern Spanish tiles. A small round window (above), with a charming wrought-iron reja, *brings extra ventilation into an upstairs bedroom.*

FLOORS, WALLS & CEILINGS

In southern Spanish houses, the natural materials from which floors, walls and ceilings are made can be seen in all their glory. Magnificent wooden beams support roofs and upper storeys; bare stone or terracotta and ceramic tiles and bricks cover floors; plaster walls are roughly painted.

A bunch of old keys giving access to the local church, hanging on a wall which has been rough-plastered and painted rusty red.

Terracotta tiles from the Spain–Gibraltar border town of Lalinea, laid slightly off-line with small, glazed, coloured inserts set in the gaps thus created. The sealant used here, linseed oil, gives the floor a deeper tone than the finish on the tiles on page 193.

Left. *A very old door formed from miscellaneous planks of wood nailed together and painted white and grey. The floor is covered with blue and white marble tiles laid in a chequerboard pattern.*

Above. *A stone floor, original to the house, has been treated with linseed oil and varnish.*

Bougainvillea sprawls elegantly across an outside wall above a terracotta wall light of typical Andalucian design based on Arab originals.

A terracotta external wall-light of a design which has been in use for centuries, painted
white like the wall behind it.

Riding hats hang on a rough-plastered and limewashed wall. The chair is an antique from Seville and the floor is covered with local tiles. In the background a horseshoe archway, its sides jutting slightly where they meet the arch itself, is painted a vibrant Andalucian blue.

These thin bricks, introduced by the Romans and still made today, were recently laid in a herringbone pattern, washed with vinegar and finished with a modern acrylic sealant to retain their pale colour. The chair is a Spanish antique and the shawl a mantón *of the type worn for processions and religious festivals.*

A magnificent and typically Andalucian ceiling built recently by the house's owner. The chestnut beams were made from trees growing on the adjoining farm which are thinned every four years.

―――――――――

Whitewashed walls support a wooden-beamed roof which has been lined with matting made from caña, *split cane, for greater warmth. Caña is found all over Spain and the matting is used not as a floor covering (it is too hard underfoot) but for blinds, roofing on terraces and, as here, as a ceiling liner.*

LIVING
SPACES

LIVING SPACES ARE SIMPLY FURNISHED,
ALMOST SPARTAN. THEIR WARMTH COMES
FROM LIGHT REFLECTED OFF WALLS PAINTED
RICH, MELLOW COLOURS OR WHITEWASHED.
BLUE IS RARELY USED BECAUSE IT SEEMS
CHILLY, BUT WHEN IT DOES APPEAR IT CREATES
A WELCOMING COOLNESS IN THIS SEARINGLY
HOT CLIMATE.

An exceptionally pretty, modern wrought-iron hanger
for kitchen implements, based on an old design and now
hung in a living room for decoration.

This seating area was created when agricultural buildings were converted into an elegant home in the late 1980s. The tiles were found in Seville, the pillars which form the legs of the table in Cortes, and the magnificent pot, once used for storing olive oil, in Lorca.

A cool, simple interior with a small sofa covered with a white linen loose cover. The floor is laid with large terracotta tiles. The effect is restrained and ascetic, the only touch of exoticism coming from the painting of a reclining woman.

An old granary, now converted and used as a meeting place for people involved in the arts in Andalucia. Rush seating is a typical feature of Spanish furniture. Pictures on the walls are collages made by the owner's mother from antique Peruvian textiles.

Maria Foixa's private sitting room. Walls are painted with glowing red pigments, the pair of painted doors is antique and an animal skin rug warms the tiled floor.

This magnificent fireplace is late nineteenth century and original to the house. On the left, the original cooking stove can just be seen. Here, a cocido, bean and lentil stew, would have simmered all day awaiting the return of hungry farm workers. The rocking chair is typically Andalucian, the bellows are from Marrakesh and the mirror and candlesticks are English.

Detail of a fireplace decorated with antique tiles. Believed originally to have lined the ceiling of a palace in Seville or Cordoba, these tiles were found in the barn of a local farm. The mantelshelf is formed from Roman bricks and the dish is Portuguese.

This type of lantern with coloured glass panels was introduced by the Moors and is still made today. Here, a modern version lights the sitting room of a casita *with electricity, but formerly such lanterns would have held candles or oil lamps.*

203

FURNITURE

FURNITURE IN ANDALUCIAN HOUSES IS
UNPRETENTIOUS: WOODEN CHAIRS USUALLY
HAVE RUSH SEATS; SMALL FOLDING CHAIRS
AND STOOLS ARE BASED ON DESIGNS
INTRODUCED BY THE MOORS AND OTHERS.
THE *MESA CAMILLA*, HOWEVER, IS EXOTIC. IT
CONSISTS OF A ROUND TABLE WITH BUILT-IN
BRAZIER FOR WARMTH ON WINTER DAYS.

A modern chair based on a traditional design with pine
frame and rush seat, painted a dark, vibrant blue.

Washstands such as this, which is made of painted pine, were used before piped water was plumbed in. The elegant pot below is a type called a cantero, *used for cooling water.*

A mesa camilla. *No houses in Andalucia have heating other than the fireplace and stove, so the family would gather round a table like this in cold weather. Hot charcoal was laid in the centre of the lower tier. A heavy tablecloth had slits around the edge, which allowed the family to put their legs under the table to enjoy the heat.*

One corner of the sitting room on page 200 showing a small folding chair, a typical example of old Spanish furniture. The inspiration for it came from the days when Arab rulers travelled around the region, carrying their furniture with them. The little table is a traditional Spanish country piece.

One end of a long stool whose antique tooled leather top is formed from an old carriage seat.

An amuga, *a form of folding stool found in Ronda. The story goes that such stools were placed on horses' backs so that ladies could ride in relative comfort.*

A pine blanket chest with pretty iron lock, standing in front of a curtained window. The chest is a typical piece of Spanish furniture; the curtains are unusual for southern Spain and are made from fabric by the English designer George Spencer.

One of a pair of kitchen cupboard doors, the open lattice allowing air to circulate.

A mosaic of small tiles, some coloured green and blue and some plain terracotta, are laid in a tray to form a table top. The tiles are actually from north Africa, the Moorish influence clear to see.

KITCHENS

KITCHENS IN SOUTHERN SPAIN TEND TO BE

BRIGHT AND CHEERFUL, WITH A WELCOMING

ATMOSPHERE CREATED BY FLAMBOYANT,

COLOURFUL CERAMICS AND CHEQUERED

PATTERNS MADE FROM TILES OF MANY

COLOURS. PANS, BASKETS, DRIED HERBS AND

ASSORTED COOKING IMPLEMENTS HANG FROM

THE CEILINGS.

Glass jars containing home-grown olives, typically
stored in brine rather than oil, and tomato sauce.

Home-grown herbs and garlic hang from the ceiling of the kitchen of an English couple who have moved permanently to Andalucia and have converted and renovated a farm and surrounding buildings. The tiles and pots are all local.

These magnificent beams supporting the roof were once a ship's timbers. The pairs of doors were found in Ronda and the pottery is all made locally in Andalucia. Herbs hanging from the ceiling include oregano, thyme and bay, alongside a string of dried, home-grown red peppers.

217

The small green and white tiles which decorate the walls of this kitchen were hand made in Seville fifteen years ago. Similar tiles are often seen facing the outside of garden fountains in Andalucia.

*China from Italy, Mexico and Spain in a white-painted plate rack. The bowl at the
bottom is rough and unglazed on the outside, and is used to allow the dough to rise
when making bread, or for standing milk in before skimming off the cream. The tiles
are modern and made in Seville, with a star design based on Arabic decoration.*

A recently painted old spice rack stores local Spanish pottery, Mexican painted gourds and, above,
glass jars containing spices.

A busy kitchen is fitted with modern equipment but nonetheless has open lattice work on the cupboard doors –
the traditional way of allowing air to circulate.

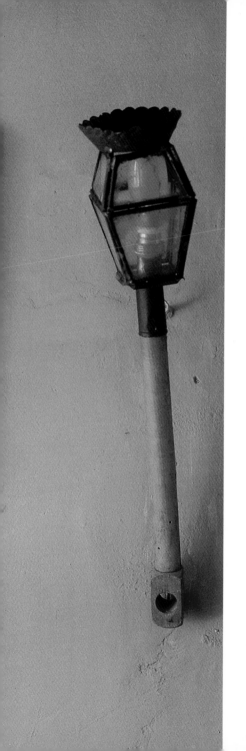

BEDROOMS
&
BATHROOMS

Bare floors and simple iron bedsteads are typical of bedrooms, which are almost invariably decorated in an unfussy style with plain painted walls and wooden ceilings. Bathrooms are cool and equally unpretentious, with white china set against brightly patterned Spanish tiles.

A small mirror is framed by antique carriage lamps on the wall of a cloakroom. The carved oak frame is one of a pair and probably once contained a picture rather than a mirror.

A Spanish iron and brass bed is covered with a much-prized English patchwork quilt. The lamp stands in what was once the corner feeding trough for beasts stabled here, bearing witness to the house's agricultural origins.

Known as the 'blue bedroom', this was once a sheep shed. The window has been made recently and fitted with a frame of chestnut wood.

Hand-painted modern tiles from Seville provide a splashback in this cloakroom.
The antique mahogany corner cupboard was found by the owner in a junk shop.

Old brass taps on a modern basin in the bathroom (left). A curved corner unit has been created using tongue-and-groove planking in the doors. The pretty blue and yellow pot is typically Andalucian.

A modern bathroom in a cottage created out of an old stable. Plain white china looks dazzlingly fresh alongside blue-painted walls and modern blue-and-white locally made tiles.

An eclectic collection of crockery crowds this dresser. Such unpretentious displays add to the warm, welcoming atmosphere of the traditional cottage.

COTTAGE
English Country Style

DETAIL IS THE KEY TO PERFECTION IN ALL THINGS, EVEN DECORATING A COTTAGE. The word 'cottage' means different things to different people, but most would agree that it is a small house, old, in the country, vernacular (built in the local style with local materials), and with a garden. Then what makes it different from a 'house'? Scale, for one thing. Inside, a cottage has small rooms, with ceilings which may be low or relatively high, depending on its age, but are always in proportion to the modest size of the rooms. A cottage also has correspondingly modest aspirations – it has no pretensions to grandeur. It is, or should be, a comfortable, practical and functional living-space.

To many people a cottage represents an ideal state of existence. As soon as you duck under the roses which ramble over the front door and pass into the cool interior, you enter another world. Here life is simple and uncluttered by the nuisances of our ordinary lives: the necessity of earning a living, finding socks that match, and dealing with the tide of unwanted paper that comes through the front door. To live in a cottage is, to the uninitiated, to escape. Even for those people who do actually live in cottages, the ideal burns bright. A friend whose welcoming cottage exudes warmth and overflows with books, pictures and possessions recently confided her own fantasy of living 'in a very simple, graceful way, with one chair, a book, a table, a vase, a picture … I could only live like that for about half-an-hour! But I like the idea.'

This ideal of simple, rural bliss is far from new. Possibly the most celebrated example is Marie-Antoinette's *Hameau* built in the grounds of the Palace of Versailles at the end of the eighteenth century. This picturesque 'hamlet' consisted of a small mill and a group of cottages, constructed with thatched roofs and distressed walls in the best theatrical scene-painting tradition. Even the woodwork was painted with cracks to create a convincing impression of age and weathering. The story goes that the fated French queen would dress in her own picturesque version of a milkmaid's garments and imagine herself an innocent rustic, released from the burden of cares and responsibilities laid upon her by an unforgiving world. Certainly she found refuge there from the stultifying formality and political intrigue of the court, whatever clothes she actually wore, and whether or not she ever milked a cow.

In England, the romantic cottage tradition was pursued equally enthusiastically, though perhaps with less extravagance. Queen Charlotte's Cottage in the grounds of what is now the Royal Botanic Gardens at Kew in London, was built in 1772. A popular summerhouse and private picnic place for the family of King George III, the cottage was sited in woodland carpeted with bluebells. The roof was thatched and the interior was decorated with paintings of cottage flowers in a scheme designed, and possibly executed, by the Princess Elizabeth, George III and Queen Charlotte's third daughter.

Queen Charlotte's Cottage is an example of the picturesque cult which caught the imagination of late eighteenth-century and early nineteenth-century English landowners, and which resulted in the construction of many a *cottage orné*. These self-consciously rustic buildings were constructed as lodges to great houses, punctuating the carefully engineered landscapes of such designers as Humphry Repton, and were also incorporated in housing schemes for farm labourers. Well-built and commodious by most contemporary cottage standards, *cottages ornés* were often lived in by genuine working people. In contrast, many much larger 'cottages' were built around the same time for the gentry and the newly rich who liked the look of them and were inspired by the idea of cottage life. Even today, some houses with the word 'cottage' in their names look more like mansions.

Generally, however, the word 'cottage' is used to describe a pretty, small-scale house, usually in the country but possibly also in a town or city; often detached from other buildings but not necessarily so. Estate agents frequently use the word, seemingly with the intention of conveying not only some idea of the property's size and scale but also implying that it possesses a certain air of solidity and quiet gentility; it is not an ex-council house, nor does it quite qualify as a grander 'residence'.

The gentility implied by the description of a building as a cottage is a fairly recent notion. For centuries, the reality of

Ann Allison worked this sampler in 1797 at the age of seventeen. Samplers often include mottoes and quotations dealing with death and God, and this one is no exception. 'How frail is human life', it gasps, 'how short the span how fleetin (sic) is (sic) days of mortal man each moment as it flies cuts short our breath and whispers in our ears prepare for death.'

life for many cottage dwellers was uncomfortable poverty. There was no sanitation, water had to be carried in, furniture was restricted to a few items, and, in the hours of darkness, heat and light were largely limited to whatever the fire or range could provide. In such a context the concept of interior decoration obviously did not exist. Life was grindingly hard work and death more likely to be the result of disease or childbirth rather than old age.

Fortunately for us, this depressing piece of history is just that – a thing of the past. Today there is hardly a cottage without central heating and a washing machine, let alone one without an indoor lavatory. In the type of cottages with which this book is concerned, any cooking apparatus that needs feeding with solid fuel is likely to be an Aga. In many cases, such traditional cookers have been superseded by halogen rings and the microwave. Decorating a cottage interior is not simply a practical necessity but provides a positive opportunity to create a home that is an expression of who you are and what kind of life you lead.

In the simplest cottage, such as a Scottish 'wee butt 'n' ben', there might be two rooms, with the front door opening directly into the first. This was originally the everyday room, used for cooking, eating, living and sleeping. Such use of the kitchen (apart from the sleeping) still prevails today. In larger houses the kitchen might once have been the domain of a servant or staff – not so in a cottage, then or now. The person doing the cooking is probably also the one who is minding the children and trying to finish the ironing in time to welcome the visitors who will sit at the kitchen table for the meal being prepared.

There is rarely space in a cottage for a whole room to be devoted to the function of a dining room – even were it wanted. A straw poll today reveals that many people, especially of the younger generations, prefer to entertain in the kitchen so that they are not excluded from the fun when serving and clearing. The kitchen is likewise a room for leisure activities such as reading the newspaper, writing letters, watching television or just sitting and talking with a glass of wine at six o'clock.

A recessed panel for a doormat, original to this Victorian cottage, takes a size of mat that is still available today. The edging is made from beaten copper, the door is painted with an off-the-shelf colour, and the fossil on the doorstep is an heirloom.

Entertaining in the kitchen epitomizes just one aspect of the informality of cottage life. A cottage is the sort of home which, far from intimidating approaching friends, invites them to open the door and walk in, after ringing the bell or knocking as a matter of courtesy. The door may be left ajar, or even wide open, in fine weather. Many cottage front doors open directly into the sitting room or kitchen – an arrangement which demands a certain agility in immediately removing muddy and wet clothes in bad weather, probably in a small space. The advantage of this layout, however, is the luxury of having warm, scented air and the sound of buzzing bees wafting directly into the sitting room or kitchen in summer.

The different types of people who are attracted to cottages vary today more than ever before. Social background no longer limits the type of building which others think it appropriate we should inhabit. Everyone can appreciate not only the charm and compact good looks which a cottage home offers, but also its practicality. Thick walls help to retain heat and resist extremes of weather. Small windows lose less heat than large ones, even if a cottage with larger windows is lighter; small windows also need less curtain fabric to keep out light and cold – that's if there are no shutters. Modestly sized rooms are quicker and cheaper to heat, especially if they also have low ceilings; they are also easier to keep clean and need less furniture. Several small rooms have an advantage over fewer large ones in that they can be dedicated to different people and purposes – a great advantage in a large or busy family. And if you leave something in your bedroom, or are tidying up after other people, you don't have to walk miles to complete the task.

Although a cottage should have no pretentions to grandeur, that does not mean to say that to be in keeping with the building's history its contents should necessarily be rough-hewn and spartan. This may have been true of poor labourers' dwellings, but some buildings that would qualify as cottages were lived in by the genteel poor: spinster aunts, gentlemen of modest means, or retired people such as rectors, housekeepers and governesses. Items of unfashionable furniture would sometimes be passed down from the big house when new were bought, to such needy people as these. An example of similar demotion comes from a grand country house, where an auctioneer discovered a complete set of Chippendale dining chairs furnishing the servants' attics – sent there in the nineteenth century when a new set (now considered less beautiful and valuable) arrived. Fine furniture of any period, along with fine pictures and objects, can look at home in a cottage, so long as their scale is compatible with the building itself.

A leg of this comfortable upholstered chair simply fell off one day, so the owner propped up the corner with a pile of paperbacks. In a lived-in cottage, such charming temporary measures tend to become permanent … The chair was upholstered in the 1970s using an Osborne and Little fabric; it may be a little grubby now, but otherwise it looks as fresh today as it did then.

Another common and invaluable source of furniture is the family. There can hardly be a cottage which is not partly furnished with cast-offs and inherited pieces, often upholstered furniture such as sofas and armchairs. And no English interior, be it a cottage or a castle, is complete without the embrace of a comfortable armchair in which to curl up by the fire at the end of a busy day. A pile of small cushions, embroidered by forebears or made up from scraps of velvet, silk and ethnic fabrics, is likely to be near at hand to guarantee your comfort. Even the tiniest cottage can accommodate a small sofa, since the English love affair with this piece of furniture results in it being made in every imaginable size, shape and style. Bedrooms often contain small upholstered chairs which were once nursery nursing chairs or 'boudoir' chairs. And often one kitchen chair, if not actually upholstered, will be made comfortable with several squashy cushions.

Keeping true both to the building and to yourself is the key to decorating a cottage. Just as no one but an extreme purist would suggest that we do without the conveniences of modern plumbing, heating, lighting or household machinery, so it would be equally absurd to insist on doing without modern materials, patterns, colours, carpets, interior sprung beds and other comforts of modern decorating and furnishing. The answer is to find a middle path, and the first step towards finding the way is gradually to educate your eye, not just in the broader view, but in the details of true cottage style. You can do this by visiting authentic old properties which are open to the public, by reading relevant books and magazines, and by developing a critical sense of what is wrong with cottages that are inappropriately decorated.

It is instructive, if a little depressing, to catalogue the horrors that are sometimes perpetrated on cottages. Fakes are the most obvious – fake wooden beams on walls and ceilings; fake stonework round fireplaces. A building should be allowed to be itself, and should never be dressed up in unconvincing tat. Varnish is often another horror, whether it appears as glossy gunge on woodwork, stonework or flag floors, or on dark stained wooden replacement windows that should be painted. Structural materials should either be left in their natural state, or plastered over where appropriate. If you visit cottages with exposed beams in the walls, you will often see that the wood has been hacked into in many places with small strokes of the hammer and chisel. This shows that the beam was once plastered over, the hacking providing a key for the plaster to grip.

Too much fuss and frills should be avoided, especially around windows; simple curtain dressing is preferable and, in many cases, shutters are better still. Too much fitted furniture can kill the interior of a cottage. Fitted bookcases and the occasional wardrobe may be suitable – they do, after all, give the maximum storage space in oddly shaped corners – but Dallas-style bedrooms are not. Garish or dreary modern colour and pattern – in pattered carpets on the floors, the fabric of upholstery and curtains, and lurid colours on painted and papered walls and tiles – is another true horror perpetrated on old cottages.

It is sad, too, to see internal doors which have been replaced at some point in the twentieth century by hollow flush doors with gaudy elaborate handles instead of knobs or latches. Doors can be replaced fairly easily, but if your doors are flush it is worth investigating to see if they

This door was recently stripped and then fed with a half-and-half mixture of linseed oil and turpentine. The turps encourages the oil to go on smoothly and sink into the wood. The rim latch is a particularly pretty example.

have panels which have simply been covered over with a piece of hardboard. If this is the case, the door within would be of solid timber so it should be heavy and fairly dull to the knock. Replacement doors should ideally be old ones. These can often be found in local auctions and sales, in reclamation yards, and by advertising in the local paper, but be aware of the size of your door openings. There was probably no such thing as a

Wood, plaster and clay tile … the timeless honesty of these fine materials
shines through countless scabby layers of old paint and the dirt of ages. This
cottage has escaped modernization and tampering in all but the most
essential ways, and consequently retains an exceptionally unspoilt
appearance and atmosphere.

'standard' size when your cottage was built, and sizes vary wildly. In the end it may be necessary to have doors custom-made, or modern solid timber doors (now available in some quite acceptable designs from DIY superstores) especially made to fit.

Metal Norfolk or Suffolk latches can be bought in any good ironmonger, and specialist suppliers of ironwork also offer some interesting designs. Brass, iron, wooden and china doorknobs can be bought new, or, even better, collected in junk shops and jumble sales. Local auctions are another possible source; if the lot includes a jumble of other architectural ironmongery, you will have to buy it all together – but you may find all kinds of old things for your home in the box or bag. Warehouses dealing in stripped pine may sell off the door furniture and other ironmongery separately. Rim latches, which sit on the surface of the door, are an attractive alternative to mortice ones, which must be embedded in the thickness of the door. The design of these has not changed in generations, and can be seen in any good ironmonger. They can also be hunted down in the same way as knobs and will sometimes be found with the original knobs still attached.

Floors can either make a room beautiful, or be an eyesore. If your boards are sound, simply feed them with linseed, stale olive or Danish oil and polish them with wax. Too much carpet, covering all floors to the edge and deadening contact with stone and wood on the ground floor, is unnecessary. Rugs, or a piece of carpet bound around the edges (any good carpet shop should do this for you), generally look better, and can easily be changed or taken with you if you move. Fitted carpet does however feel less inappropriate in a bedroom than in most other rooms, and is useful where the existing boards are not in good enough condition to leave bare, even around the edge of a room. Grass matting is more sympathetic than carpet to the age and style of old cottages and is now widely available in a range of colours and patterned weaves.

Poor boards can, however, usually be repaired and painted. If you can't obtain floor paint in a suitably subtle colour it is possible to make an emulsion-painted floor fairly hardwearing by the addition of many layers of matt or satin floor varnish. And real linoleum (as opposed to vinyl) which is made in a kaleidoscope of rich colours, makes a practical floorcovering in a kitchen, scullery/laundry, bathroom or any other 'messy' room. Flagstones can often be rescued, with work, from layers of asphalt and concrete. If they are beyond saving, tiles of many types and even concrete slabs can successfully replace them. These can be laid in a dark-and-light chequerboard pattern and polished with wax to make a sympathetic floor, hardwearing and with a lively but suitably authentic appearance.

The cottages photographed for this book have been decorated with enthusiasm and imagination by their owners. The materials used are not always old-fashioned but have been chosen for their empathy with the buildings. Some traditional materials, such as distemper and old-style emulsion paints, have recently become more readily available as a result of renewed interest in old buildings and authentic decorative materials and techniques. The National Trust range of paints is manufactured in England by the only company still in full-scale production of distemper. The paint is made with casein (an environmentally-friendly binder derived from whey of milk) as opposed to the commonly used acrylic binders, resulting in a gloriously soft, chalky finish. Some of their subtle, glowing colours can be seen in the photographs here.

The colours used in these cottages vary hugely, from white and delicate stripes to rich, strong ochre, red, green and blue, but they are never brilliant. Floors are polished, tiled or painted, covered with rush matting, old kelims and rugs, but are never concealed beneath wall-to-wall carpeting. Kitchens are rarely fitted, unless you count the sink unit. Furniture comes from all periods, as do pictures and china, and the periods all combine successfully because everything has been chosen with love and care by people for whom no detail is too small. For the same reason, valuable antiques happily coexist with jumble sale bargains and high street purchases.

Wherever there is practical space in these houses, you will find treasures on display. Many cottages have thick walls which result in deep windowsills – ideal for display, except where there are shutters. Plates can be hung on walls and china and objects arranged along the tops of cupboards, in bookshelves, or on mantelshelves. Pictures will always look better if arranged as a scheme for the whole room, rather than being dotted about at random. If you have only a few, small pictures, hang one above another, or several in a group. If they share a characteristic, such as subject matter or colour range, or if they are painted or drawn in the same medium, the group will be all the more interesting.

The statement 'books do furnish a room', made famous by the novelist Anthony Powell, is undoubtedly true. Books can also take a room over with alarming speed unless they are well organized, but no home ever feels complete without them. An alcove or recess, an entire wall or even a whole room can be lined with bookshelves, with the furniture placed in front. As well as being attractive, books provide some insulation against sound, a bonus if your cottage has partition walls which are barely more than boards.

Lighting in a cottage, as in any house, needs to be practical as well as visually pleasing. Pendant lightbulbs in the middle of ceilings are rarely attractive, and in a cottage with low ceilings they can be dangerously impractical. Many people deplore modern spotlights and downlighters, including the author Hugh Lander, whose books on cottages are a rich source of information and delight. In certain circumstances, however, they are a practical option, and if cleverly placed they may be aesthetically innocuous.

Sunlight casts a dramatic shadow through the back of this Windsor chair on to the plain white-painted plaster behind. Dark wood against white walls provides a clean, bold contrast which sums up the fresh simplicity of English cottage style.

An alternative is to use wall brackets, but these too can be unsatisfactory, both in appearance and when they interfere with furniture, bookshelving or picture arrangements. Lamps on tables are almost always the best solution in cottages, but to be totally practical at least one in each room should be wired to switch on at the door – a requirement which can cause difficulties. It is best to take each room individually and work out a tailor-made solution to the problem of lighting.

242

The fireplace is a vital source of visual comfort in English cottages in winter, as well as a source of heat. A crackling fire is ideal, whether in a grate or a stove, but sometimes it is preferable or necessary to have a gas fire. This could be a real-effect fire (now so convincing it is difficult to tell the difference at a glance) although these do not provide heat as efficiently as the real thing. A gas-fired stove will give a roaring heat and look convincing too.

Central heating is another modern convenience which needs careful thought. If radiators are already in position and there is no question of changing them, paint them the same colour as the walls for minimum intrusion. It might be possible to change some of your slightly antiquated 'modern' radiators for new ones which may be a fraction of the size but equally (or more) thermally efficient. If you are installing a completely new system, consider choosing cast-iron radiators, which take longer to become hot but retain the heat for longer. These are available in some traditional designs, and in simple modern designs which can look appropriate in old buildings.

If you treat your cottage home as a friend it will surely repay the compliment. Consider in detail its character, and enjoy it, don't fight it. Dress it considerately, not only to reflect your personality and lifestyle, your taste and preferences, but also bearing in mind the age of your home, its natural form and features. Make the most of what it is, rather than trying to make it look like something it is not. Each of the interiors of the cottages shown here is practical and, above all, personal. Each has been built up gradually, sympathetically, on a budget and without the help of interior designers. Their inhabitants have decorated them in such a way that they are irresistibly inviting. The country cottages shown in this book have been chosen to provide you with inspiration and a rich source of new ideas. We hope that after reading this book you will find that you are seeing with new eyes, and that no cottage will ever look quite the same again.

DOORS & WINDOWS

DOORS AND WINDOWS ARE THE EYES, EARS

AND LUNGS OF A HOUSE. THE WAY THEY

LOOK AND FEEL — THEIR STYLE AND THE

MATERIALS FROM WHICH THEY ARE MADE,

THEIR PAINTED OR POLISHED FINISHES,

THEIR KNOBS AND CATCHES — IS VITAL TO

THE APPEARANCE OF A COTTAGE HOME.

Old rim latches, which sit on the surface of the door rather than being fitted into its thickness, can be picked up in junk shops and markets. When cleaned, painted and oiled inside, they should give good service. New rim latches are still available from ironmongers.

This pitch pine door, complete with stock lock with pierced iron mounts, was found being used to restrain hay in a barn. The current owners, who were renovating their cottage at the time, rescued it and had a doorway specially altered to fit. The keys are old but do not match the lock.

An idiosyncratic cat-door. A round hole was cut in the wood and the portcullis-style door added on the inside, with a bolt to keep it open when the family, and cat, are in residence.

This old plank door was installed in the 1970s to separate the kitchen from the larder beyond. The larder also has a door, which leads into the garden, so the iron loop below the Suffolk latch is intended to secure the kitchen against unwanted intruders.

A narrow ledge above a doorway is a good place on which to display small objects and pictures. The wool picture is the work of a sailor and is part of a collection, one of which incorporates the sailor's hatband showing the name of his ship. The bottles are salt glazed and would have been used to hold inks or dyes.

An old wrought iron casement window latch with a curly tail makes a charming change from most bland modern window furniture.

Bare Camel-stone mullions frame leaded lights in this east-facing window. The leadwork was replaced ten years ago by a local craftsman, found through the local business telephone directory. The glass bottles were dug up in the garden.

Roses arranged in a Victorian china boot on a sunny white-painted windowsill. A few leaves of ivy can be seen through the window. In the garden below, copper leafed cherry trees stand out against the delicate foliage of silver poplars, with lush English countryside stretching into the distance.

HALLS, STAIRS & FLOORS

FLAGSTONES, POLISHED OR PAINTED
BOARDS, RUGGED POTTERY TILES, EXOTIC
RUGS ON RUSH MATTING, THE SCARRED
TREADS OF AN OLD STAIRCASE . . . THE
FEEL AND LOOK OF WHAT IS UNDERFOOT
MAKES ALL THE DIFFERENCE TO A HOME.
COTTAGE HALLS, FLOORS AND STAIRS ARE
UNPRETENTIOUS AND SIMPLY FURNISHED.

These stairs lead from the ground to the first floor. A
flight from the first to second floors is oak, but this lower
flight was apparently replaced in the nineteenth century
with these lightweight treads and risers. The tongue and
groove dado was probably added at the same time.

Coats, hats, gloves, scarves, boots, a basket, umbrellas and miscellaneous sporting equipment jostle for position in a typical cottage hallway which doubles as a cloakroom. No English country hall is complete without an umbrella stand to receive umbrellas still dripping with rain, and a flagstone floor is likewise ideal for a hall in this damp climate.

The ideal cottage has a garden. This seventeenth- century flagstone hall floor is the natural indoor resting place for gardening clutter, including early-twentieth-century galvanized watering cans and a pair of workmen's clogs from Brittany. The owner claims that these are ideal gardening footwear in the damp English climate, keeping one's feet both dry and comfortable.

The stairs in this Victorian cottage rise straight up between two walls, from just inside the front door, to a tiny landing at the top. The wall, skirting and stairs have all been painted with paints from the National Trust range, based on colours in historic houses: emulsion has been used on the wall, with dead flat (matt) oil applied to skirting, treads and risers.

This beautiful oak staircase looks entirely at home in a seventeenth-century cottage in Suffolk, even though it is actually a modern adaptation. The bare wood has not been covered with unnecessary carpet.

The threshold of a room showing old, stained and dirty boards on one side, and similar boards which have been painted on the other. Emulsion-painted boards have been sealed and made fairly hardwearing by applying layer upon layer of satin varnish, but special floor paints could also be used.

An original floor such as this is a treasure beyond compare which cannot be reproduced today. The sheen on its surface is the result of centuries of polishing and use and its dusky colour is caused by the natural darkening of oak exposed to sunlight. The boards are made from seasoned oak and each is 30 cm (12 in) wide.

Yorkshire flagstones have been cut into squares and set diagonally within a rectangular frame to create this pretty hall floor.

The flagstone floor of this kitchen is original to the cottage, built in 1877. The owners removed layers of vinyl flooring, asphalt and concrete to reveal the flags beneath. They are untreated, their patina being the result of much use by adults and small children. Occasionally they are scrubbed. The chair was found in a mill sale.

PAINT

COLOURS IN THE ENGLISH COTTAGE VARY GREATLY, FROM WHITE TO THE RICH TONES OF OCHRE, RED, GREEN AND BLUE WHICH INTRODUCE WARMTH AND LIFE ON RAINY DAYS AND GLOW IN THE SUMMER SUNSHINE. TYPES OF PAINT INCLUDE ORIGINAL WHITEWASH, MODERN ACRYLICS AND OLD-FASHIONED DISTEMPER, IN FASHION AGAIN.

Pitted layers of tinted whitewash and plaster have taken on an abstract, almost sculptural, quality. Each colour was mixed individually, the blue shades being made with a powder known in Yorkshire as 'dolly blue' which was added to laundry to make it blue-white.

A wonderfully distressed, painted wooden plank door with sneck-latch (the sneck is the curved lever which lifts the latch), reveals centuries of decorative attention and wear. A similarly dramatic effect could be achieved by an enthusiastic amateur or a specialist decorator.

The upstairs of this cottage is now a home for doves, one of whom favours a wall-mounted, rush-seated chair as a comfortable place to sit. Layers of paint on the walls have crumbled to reveal the many different colours applied over generations.

*Emulsion (on walls) and dead flat (matt) oil paints from the National Trust range – here Berrington Blue and
Book Room Red. Both shades are well-suited to this Victorian cottage. The blue is a copy of a mid-nineteenth-
century colour found in the boudoir at Berrington Hall in Hereford and Worcester; the red is also mid-nineteenth-
century and is derived from paint found at Attingham Park in Shropshire.*

A comfortable wooden chair casts a shadow on an original studwork partition wall in a seventeenth-century Somerset cottage. When artists James and Kate Lynch bought the house this wall was whitewashed; James toned down the modern paints with varnish mixed with small quantities of burnt umber, yellow ochre and black artist's oil paint.

The plaster between the external studwork on the lower part of this wall is new and unpainted. It was applied as usual and then brushed to look rough and old.

A collection of Victorian jelly moulds, glass bottles dug up in the garden and a bulbous fly catcher gleam against a painted wall. The rich green is a mixture of standard off-the-shelf colours. The collection of glassware is arranged on oak shelves, formerly used as a pan rack, screwed to the wall.

*A soft, strong red provides a rich background for these four pictures, mounted in
wood and gilt frames. Each has a family connection, having been drawn, stitched
or painted by the owner's forebears. They are more visually interesting grouped in
this way than they would be if dotted around the walls of the room.*

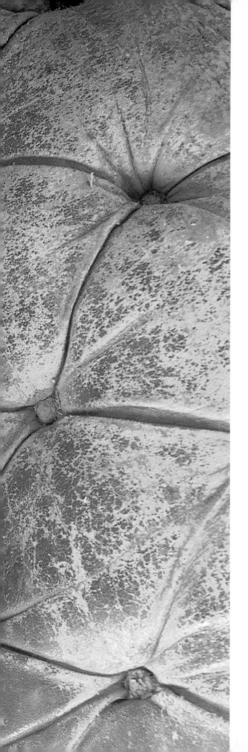

PATTERN

BEAMED CEILINGS CREATE A PATTERN IN
THEMSELVES, WHICH CHANGES TO A
THREE-DIMENSIONAL PUZZLE WHEN THE
CEILING IS OPENED TO THE EVES.
ELSEWHERE, PRINTED AND WOVEN
FABRICS, PATCHWORK, CROCHET AND
CROSS-STITCH BRING APPLIED PATTERN
INTO THE COTTAGE INTERIOR.

Cushions covered with pieces of kelim are piled up on a
battered leather-covered chesterfield. The sofa's
upholstery buttons make a geometric pattern of their
own, while the soft brown of the leather provides the
delicious vegetable-dye colours of the cushions with a
harmonious background.

The brilliantly-coloured crocheted shawl which livens up this dull sofa is an heirloom, made by the owner's great-grandmother. She made a different shawl for each of her three grandchildren and seven great-grandchildren. What is like oak panelling behind the sofa is actually an original elm studwork partition. The other side of this wall is shown in the upper illustration on page 267.

This cushion looks as if it is generations old but was actually made by the house owner's mother-in-law. The chair is a particularly pretty example of a nineteenth-century spindleback.

After decades of use, the colours are fading and the weave of this linen union is showing through the printed pattern. This is a detail of the loose cover on an upholstered armchair. Floral patterned fabric has been an essential element in many a typical English interior, at least since the Victorian mania for flowers.

The elaborate geometric pattern and brilliant colours of this kelim enliven a cottage sitting room. Originating from the Van area of south eastern Anatolia, the rug is around sixty years old and is laid on Indian hemp matting. This in turn covers a floor of which part is concrete and part wooden boards.

275

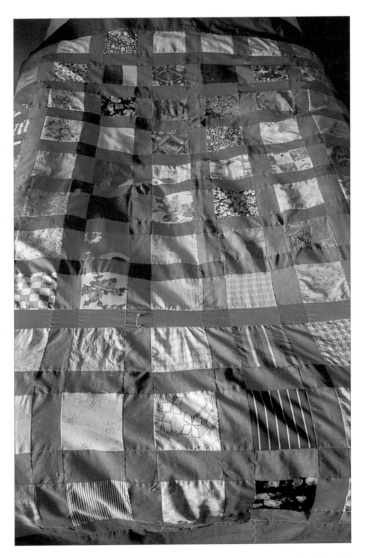

The rich colours and rigid geometric pattern of this Victorian patchwork quilt make a strong impact in this dark, low-ceilinged bedroom.

The red-and-white striped cover on this painted iron bedstead is dramatic and modern-looking. It is actually Victorian, bought in County Durham in the north of England, and is extremely warm, consisting of two layers, one cotton and one woollen. Each stripe is a separate piece of cotton sewn to the next.

Pattern need not be applied – here the structural members of a magnificent beamed roof make a three-dimensional geometric design. The spaces between have been plastered up to the eaves and painted ochre, a strong colour that tones well with the golden brown of the wood.

FURNITURE

All types of furniture look at home in a cottage — from the rugged and worn rustic chair to a huge bookcase, made specially to fit the space. Upholstered chairs and sofas are cosy and welcoming; cupboards are invaluable. Apparently grand furniture may not be all it seems.

This Windsor chair was once stained black but the stain has worn away in the places where the chair has had most use – on the seat and on the arms – allowing the golden colour and pretty grain of the beech to show through.

Above. *This imposing oak dresser is actually a 'marriage' of bits and pieces of furniture. The 1701 date plate is detachable. Dark, glossily polished wood makes a magnificent background for this collection of china which includes pieces by Wedgwood, Ashworth, Rockingham and Spode, as well as by the contemporary potter Juliet Beaumont. A mug made by her hangs on a brass cup hook decorated with a face* (right).

Above. *An old painted cupboard,
rescued from the potting shed of a
friend who was moving house,
makes a magical still life, piled up
with terracotta flower pots.*
Left. *Three separate pieces of
furniture, none of them grand, are
piled on top of each other to
magnificent effect in this high-
ceilinged Victorian cottage. The
small chest of drawers on top holds
treasures; the big chest of drawers
was found in the house, hidden
behind fitted furniture.*

The arm of a wonderfully worn leather-covered chesterfield sofa, showing the elaborate detailing of the ruched and piped upholstery.

One corner of this sitting room is dominated by a bookcase and armchair (see also page 235). The bookcase was made especially for the space by a local joiner and painted to match the walls. The floor is also painted, and the rug was bought from a village sale for a few pounds.

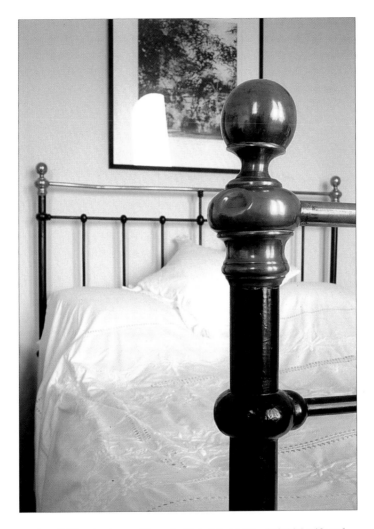

A small Victorian iron and brass double bed, just 1.35m (4 ft 6 in) wide and draped in white, is in keeping with the scale and simplicity of this airy cottage. The bed was found in a London auction. The wallpaper is a delicate pink-and-white stripe from Laura Ashley.

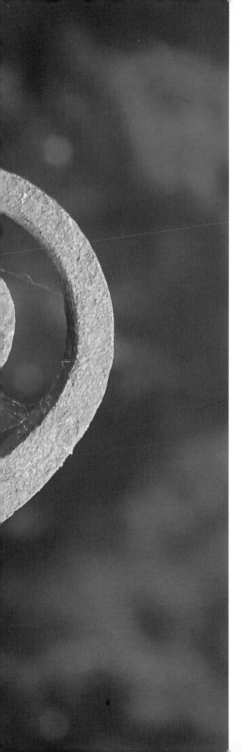

THE
FIREPLACE

A ROARING FIRE OR GLOWING STOVE IS
THE FOCUS OF A ROOM, ESPECIALLY
DURING THE COLD WET MONTHS OF AN
ENGLISH WINTER. THE HEART REJOICES IN
TEA, OR A HOT TODDY, TAKEN SITTING BY
THE FIRE. THE MANTELPIECE, MEAN-
WHILE, IS A USEFUL PLACE FOR
MISCELLANEOUS POSSESSIONS AND
POSTCARDS.

Fire dogs are free-standing supports for logs in a large open hearth known as a down hearth. This one has a curly heart-shaped end.

This type of wide open fireplace, known as a down hearth, is most people's ideal of a cottage fireside. Warm and welcoming, it also provides the room with a visual focus. The fire is built on free-standing fire dogs, but it could equally well be made in a fire basket in this sort of hearth. The mantelshelf inevitably collects miscellaneous clutter. The room's furniture and decorations are refreshingly austere.

This stove is a gas-powered modern version of a Victorian design, and is not too big in appearance for the scale of the room while giving out plenty of heat. The pot is round-bottomed and African, with an imprinted pattern. The dried roses and cache-pot were found in a village sale. The hearth is covered with black quarry tiles.

Above. *A wonderful jumble of possessions on a mantelshelf, including old matchboxes, clay pipes, a doll, pottery and a candlestick.*

Right. *This carved overmantel is another 'marriage' (see dresser on page 280), this time of a Victorian centre panel and two older grotesque figures. The cups and saucers commemorate royal events, the jug and candlesticks are English and the shells were found in Africa.*

Detail of a late eighteenth- or early nineteenth- century cast-iron hob-grate in a cottage in Somerset. The bars of the fire basket are wrought iron and could be made to any length, for an exact fit across the width of the hearth.

A battered, copper chestnut roaster with a wonderful patina of age. Its curved cut-out pattern is reminiscent of a fossil form.

An extraordinary pair of fireside bellows, operated with a foot-pump action, looks like a strange and wonderful creature that might lift its head and walk away at any moment. Other fireside paraphernalia can be seen in the background.

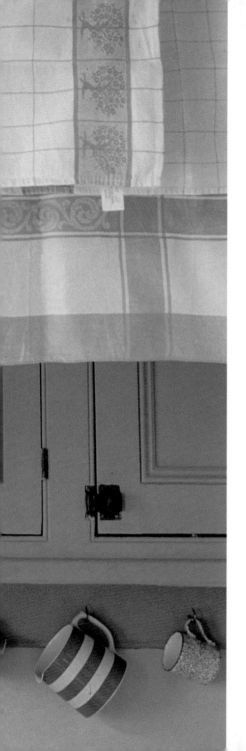

KITCHENS
&
BATHROOMS

The cottage kitchen is a warm, friendly place, where an old dresser rubs shoulders with an AGA or second-hand gas cooker. It is rarely fitted out in the latest technology; rather, it exudes old-fashioned charm, while displaying garlic, olive oil and spices on its shelves.

These storage cupboards are original to the cottage. They support a row of mugs including some Cornish Kitchenware and some Spode Blue Italian. Tea towels and tablecloth (all second-hand or high-street purchases) dry on a creel suspended from the ceiling.

A mass of kitchen china, collected over thirty-five years, crowds this primitive dresser. Some pieces have been brought from France and Italy, but most are English. Nothing matches, and the collection is designed for use (breakages are regrettable but not mourned) rather than display. Patches of the clay lump walls can be seen behind.

294

Miscellaneous picturesque kitchen utensils hanging from cup hooks under a fishy collection. They include a rabbit chocolate mould, egg slicer, mincer and barbecue tongs. The green enamel object was an iron stand, for placing the iron on when you took it off the fire. If you filled it with coals it could also help keep the iron hot.

Blue and white china has an enduring charm, and none more so than this classic striped design known as Cornish Kitchenware. It is still made in Derbyshire, where it originated in the early twentieth century, by the company T. G. Green of Church Gresley.

Most of the cottages in this book have unfitted
kitchen. Here, a second-hand gas cooker
stands next to the bottom half of a 1930s pre-
utility dresser with useful enamel worktop.
Ingredients like olive oil have now joined
Marmite as staples of English food.

Above. *This magnificent cottage range is no
longer used for cooking, but it keeps the
kitchen warm and is a useful incinerator for
disposable nappies. The design was mass
produced in the second half of the nineteenth
century and was especially popular in the
north of England.*

A cottage breakfast table, with tea, brown bread and home-made jam in the kitchen of woven-textile designer Georgina Cardew. The table was painted and decorated with emulsion and then varnished.

An elderly porcelain sink with integral draining board is still in use, with updated plumbing. Rubber tap spouts are invaluable and cost little from ironmongers and village stores. This cottage is on a hill, so the ground drops away steeply from the front door while the kitchen at the back is below ground level.

This bath and basin with their handsome taps were in the cottage when it was bought in the eighties. Old taps and bathroom china usually cost a fraction of the price of new, and can be tracked down in markets and through advertisements in local papers, parish magazines and post office windows.

Light reflects off white-painted tongue-and-groove partitioning and a panelled door opening on to cellar steps. Gloss paint can help reflect light into darkish corners of cottage kitchens, as can mirrors hung on walls, and solid door panels replaced with glass.

Shells collected on summer holidays in Scotland have here been piled up on the sill of a bathroom window, in front of a seaside painting made by a friend. The modern net curtain gives a fresh and airy feel to the composition.

ACKNOWLEDGEMENTS

DEDICATION

To the doctors, nurses and staff of the Paediatric Oncology Department and Children's Day Hospital at St James's University Hospital in Leeds, with thanks.

Elizabeth Hilliard would like to thank the many people whose kindness and enthusiasm have helped her with this book, but she is especially grateful to the following:

Charles Allen; Emma Armitage; M. and Mme Pierre Rosetti Balanesco; Kate Bell; June Bellamy; Veronique Blum; Felicity Bryan and Michele Topham; Paul Burcher; Contessa Capponi; Katrin Cargill; Georgina Cardew and Philip Austen; Conran Octopus for the extract from *Terence Conran's France*; Christopher Corr; Wendy Dallas; M. and Mme d'Annuzio; Malcolm and Ann Davison; E. Jane Dickson; the *Ecomusée* at St Dégan en Brec'h; Helen Selka Farmiloe; Maria Foixa; T. G. Green; Ros and Martin Hart; Annet Held; Tom Helme; Karen Hill; Mrs David Hilliard; Historic Royal Palaces; Karen Humphries and Simon Rose; Alan James; Rachel King; Laurence Krzyzanek; Hugh Lander; Mme Henri Laurent; Olivia Lowsley-Williams; James and Kate Lynch; Tessa Mackay; Barbara Mellor and Gavin Harding; Ilaria Miani; Angus Mitchell; Tom Bell and Amparo Garrido; National Trust Paints; Diana Paget; Annabel Park; Morten and Julia Pedersen; Christina Probert Jones; Sarah Riddick; Charlotte Scott; William Selka; Maria Jose Sevilla; Souleiado; Lucy Stewart-Roberts and Christopher Hollis; Elisabeth de Stroumillo; Emanuela Stucchi Prinetti; Helen Sudell; Susan Taylor; Nick Tudor; Mr and Mrs Nicholas Walter; Mrs David Waterhouse; Maryanne Wilkins; Rebecca Willis; Anna Wright.

Above all, she thanks John Miller, whose beautiful photographs make this book what it is.